A Pictorial Tribute to the

BRISTOL OMNIBUS
COMPANY

and ASSOCIATED FLEETS

1936–1983

This early 1950s view taken at Swindon gives a fair representation of the buses in the Bristol Tramways fleet at the time. On the left is No. 2110 (BHU 966), which has a 1935 JNW chassis and is fitted with a Gardner 5LW engine, a low PV2 radiator and a 1948 pattern Bristol B35R body *(see Plates 27 & 44)*. The bus was transferred to Gloucester City and renumbered 1295 in 1957, being withdrawn in 1959. Next to No. 2110 is No. 3034 (CHW 45), a 1936 GO5G which was fitted with a PV2 radiator and a new ECW H56R body in 1949, one of nearly 100 Gs so treated *(see Plate 54)*. It was withdrawn in 1955, the ECW body then being paired to a wartime K6A chassis to form bus No. 3786 (HHY 587) — *see Plate 112*. The double decker on the right is No. 3673 (JHT 122), a 1946 K5G with a 'relaxed utility' Duple H56R body *(see Plate 35)*. In 1956 this body was replaced by an ECW H56R body, identical to that carried here by No. 3034. The resultant combination was added to the Gloucester City fleet as No. 1546, remaining in service until 1965. Poking its nose in at the back of this line-up is No. 2363 (AHW 536), a 1934 J that had received a 5LW in 1946 and the ECW B35R body shown in 1949 *(see Plate 57)*. After withdrawal in 1955, the ECW body was transferred to a 1941 L5G, No. 2165 (HAE 15) — *see Plate 120*.

R. F. Mack

Frontispiece: Seventeen years separate the entry into service of these two ECW-bodied Bristol double deckers, yet there is a strong 'family resemblance' showing that a good design does not 'date'. The older bus is No. C8374 (WHW 815), a 1956 KSW6G with a Gardner 6LW engine, 'crash' gearbox and sixty seat open platform body. It is being passed by No. C5028 (MHW 295L), a 1973 VRT/SL6G with a Gardner 6LXB engine, semi-automatic transmission and seventy seat dual-doorway

Allan Macfarlane

...ined up at Trowbridge, in 1979, are five very different buses to represent that era. The double decker on the ...3 (HTC 729N), a 1975 VRT/SL6G with H70F bodywork; Nos. 5503 and 5502 were the only double deckers ... ...e's strength at the time *(see Plates 181—184 and 216)*. Next comes No. 427 (SWS 773S), a 1978 B43F-bodied LH6L, one of nearly 100 in the fleet, most of which had a rather short life *(see Plates 218 & 249)*. In the centre is No. 1099 (RHT 148G) which is a B53F-bodied RELL6L, new in 1968 and the 100th such bus to join the fleet in eighteen months! *(See Plate 167)*. The bus alongside it is No. 558 (GEU 370N), a 1975 Leyland National of the short variety, seating B44F *(see Plate 212)*. The bus on the right of the view is particularly interesting as it is one of the last two MWs in the fleet, both of which ended their days at Trowbridge, shortly after this photograph was taken. They were Nos. 2589 & 2590 (982 UHW & 983 UHW), MW5Gs of 1964 with B45F bodies, No. 2590 being seen here.

Allan Macfarlane

A Pictorial Tribute to the

BRISTOL OMNIBUS
COMPANY

and ASSOCIATED FLEETS

1936–1983

Allan Macfarlane

Oxford Publishing Co.

Copyright © 1985 Oxford Publishing Co.

ISBN 0-86093-342-3

Typesetting by:
Aquarius Typesetting Services, New Milton, Hants.

Printed in Great Britain by:
Balding + Mansell Ltd., Wisbech, Cambs.

Published by:
Oxford Publishing Co.
Link House
West Street
POOLE, Dorset

Foreword

To me, this book is the manifestation of a long-standing ambition. I have spent a lifetime observing the Bristol Company's buses, and have accrued quite an intense knowledge of them. I am grateful for the chance to impart my wealth of information to you, the reader!

Bristol's fleet, over the years, has contained immense variety and I have tried to reflect many of its unique aspects within these pages. It has a tradition of being an interesting company in the enthusiasts' eyes, often coming up with the unexpected; not that the bus company deliberately tries to instil excitement in the bus fanatic! They are there to provide an all-important, all too often criticised service, as economically as possible.

I have endeavoured to be impartial in my selection of views, despite having personal preferences. I started travelling by bus to school in 1950 on the Clevedon local 25D. The buses on this service included very new MHW-registered Ls which were the ultimate in Bristol's half-cab saloons. This doubtless accounts for my affection for the L type. Frequent visits to Bristol were undertaken on the smoky top deck of a 1948 K6A or K6B on route 25, and Bristol at the time presented an ever-growing fleet of KSWs which soon became personal favourites too; so much so that during their final years, in the early 1970s, my good friend Graham Jones and I formed the KSW Club, to keep tabs on them for the benefit of other enthusiasts. Recently, in order to widen the identity of our society, we have revived the name of 'The Bristol Interest Circle'.

It is to the members of the original Bristol Interest Circle, active from 1938 and through the 1940s and 1950s, that I owe my greatest debt, for passing on information, over the years, on which I have drawn in preparing this book. My gratitude is extended to Peter Hulin, George Vowles, Peter Davey, Mike Mogridge and the late D. C. Howell for several items of historical information, and in particular to Mike Tozer for 25 years in which he has willingly and frequently volunteered information. My thanks also go to Dave Withers, Geoff Bruce, Mike Walker and Martin Curtis who have helped me to keep up to date with occurrences in the fleet. The publications of The PSV Circle are acknowledged as valuable reference works. To my other 'bus' friends, I extend a general 'Thanks!'.

I have made a point of utilising, as far as is possible, the work of our local photographers, whose names appear throughout the book; their help is greatly appreciated, as is that of all others who have permitted me to use their pictures. I am obliged to Roy Gingell and Dave Withers, who have allowed me free access to the Bristol Vintage Bus Group photographic collection.

Finally, special thanks go to my wife, Anne, for patiently enduring the isolation I requested while preparing this book, and for her valuable assistance in checking the phraseology and grammar.

Allan Macfarlane
Westbury-on-Trym
May 1984

Introduction

The origin of intensive passenger transport in the City of Bristol goes back to 1871, when the idea of providing a tramway service caught the City Council's imagination. However, the Corporation soon ran into problems of financing the proposed tramway, and even when construction of the first line was started, in the summer of 1873, it took nine months to complete. The line ran from the top of Colston Street and along Whiteladies Road, to the foot of Blackboy Hill. Upon completion, a group of local citizens decided to act and negotiated with the Corporation for the lease of the line, upon which their company would operate the trams. With discussions successfully concluded, the Bristol Tramways Company was brought into being at the end of 1874. The Secretary was George White, who later became Chairman and very much the driving force behind the Company.

The first route opened to the public in August 1875, accompanied by the usual ceremonies and luncheons. It proved to be very well-used, particularly by those wishing to take the airs on The Downs. The rails were extended in December to run down Colston Street (by way of a problematical hairpin bend at the top) to St. Augustine's Parade, in the heart of the city, beside the harbour. In later years, this was to form the hub of the tramway system and became known as the Tramways Centre, Nowadays, forty years after the last tram ran, it is still called 'The Centre',
and the old title can be heard, on occasions, even now.

The opening of new routes forged ahead, covering all main roads out of the central area and in 1880, the Company purchased the original track from the Corporation. In the same year, a short trial was conducted with a steam tram locomotive hauling a horse-car, but it was electric traction several years later that was to mark the end of the horse-trams. The entire system was electrified between 1895 and 1900.

Meanwhile, in 1886, following the Tramway Company's activities in buying up various cab owners and related businesses, an offshoot was formed entitled the Bristol Cab Company. This company not only had the monopoly of hansoms, hackneys, etc., but also inherited all the city's funeral undertakings!

The Bristol Cab Company and the Bristol Tramways Company merged, in 1887, to form a new company — The Bristol Tramways & Carriage Company Ltd. Significantly, the same year saw the first regular horse-bus service commence in the city. The influential residents of Clifton had successfully halted a proposal to build a branch of the Whiteladies Road tramway through to the Clifton Suspension Bridge, but accepted this horse-bus 'feeder' service. Before long, feeder services were being provided to other areas.

Eventually, the arrival of the internal combustion engine

After their 1906—1910 deliveries, Bristol Tramways only renewed their interest in double deckers in the early 1930s. Weston-super-Mare had the distinction of receiving several of the early Bristol G types including this bus, which arrived in the first month of 1936. No. G137 (CAE 865) had a 52 seat Bristol body, painted in the smart dark blue and white livery. Under the 1937 fleet renumbering scheme the bus became 3020, and received a Gardner 5LW oil engine in 1939, in place of its six cylinder petrol unit. The bus stands here at the Grand Pier on route 152, which ran the entire length of the seafront.

George Vowles

The following four photographs help to illustrate a feature for which the Bristol Company was famous . . . the rebodying of buses and their consequent longevity. The bus shown in each view is No. 2082 (FAE 56), which was significant in being the very first Bristol L type, having chassis number L5G.43.1. It entered service in May 1938, bearing a Bristol B32D body, and is shown in its original condition *(above)*. This photograph was taken in the early days of the war, in Grange Court Road, alongside the Westbury-on-Trym depot.

George Vowles

During the early post-war rebodying programme, eight pre-war L5Gs were chosen to receive new Bristol bodies, in 1949, at the same time being given low radiators. No. 2082 was the second to be treated, and is shown *(below)* at Weston-super-Mare. The new body was to B33D layout and still featured hinged doors at the top of the entrance steps.

Bristol Vintage Bus Group Collection

The 1949 Bristol bodies on the eight pre-war L5Gs did not have a particularly long life. As early as 1956/7, five of them were replaced, either by 1949 ECW bodies or by 1950/1 Bristol bodies. The replacement units had been built on reconditioned J chassis which, by the mid-1950s, were beginning to tire. These metal-framed bodies, however, had a lot of service left in them, so they were transferred to a variety of pre-war and post-war Ls. In June 1957, No. 2082 thereby gained its third body, which was a 1951 Bristol B35R unit, removed from No. 2062 (EHT 546). The bus is seen *(above)* at Grand Parade, Bath.

P. R. Forsey

Only four months after receiving the 1951 body, No. 2082 re-entered the workshops and was converted for one man operation. This entailed the building of an entrance at the front, panelling in the rear doorway, and cutting out the bulkhead to enable the driver to collect the fares. No. 2082 was one of the first treated and is seen *(below)* on the forecourt of Highbridge depot. The story does not end here, as in 1961, to make way for the renumbering of the coach fleet, No. 2082 was renumbered 2303. It was withdrawn in January 1962, but then saw a year's further service with the well-known Essex operator, MacGregor of Sible Hedingham. FAE 56 had the indignity of becoming a mobile chip shop before finally being scrapped in 1965.

George Vowles

resulted in the development of the motor bus. In January 1906, Bristol's first motor buses commenced work, on the Suspension Bridge route. The vehicles were 35 seat, double deck Thornycrofts, part of a batch of twelve. The top deck of the early double deckers proved unpopular and, subsequently, the seats were removed; after that, no double deckers featured in the bus fleet until the 1930s. However, one of the competitors, Greyhound Motors, successfully ran London-type AEC NSs in Bristol during the 1920s.

The use of motor buses coincided with extensions outside Bristol to nearby towns, including a connection with the Bath Company's trams. Charabanc tours were first offered in 1907. All was not well with the motor bus fleet, however, and in particular with some buses of Fiat origin. The buses were found to be unreliable on Bristol's hilly terrain (BT&CC won a court action against the suppliers of the Fiat chassis, for supplying vehicles not in accordance with the Company's specification), so the enterprising BT&CC decided to build its own complete vehicles, this proving to be a very wise move. The first vehicles of Bristol manufacture — 16 seat type C40 single deckers — took over on the Clifton route in May 1908, and the Company never looked back! They were able to provide nearly all their own buses before the outbreak of World War I, by which time over 100 'Bristols' were running for the Company. Additionally, a few had been supplied to related firms.

Construction of buses was undertaken at Filton, just to the north of the city, until the Chairman, the enterprising and forceful Sir George White, decided to start building aeroplanes — another very successful move. The Bristol Aeroplane Company (BAC) was formed in 1910, and Filton was chosen as its home. With the arrival of hostilities, aircraft design advanced rapidly, with Bristol producing many of the most successful fighters. In subsequent years, Bristol not only made world-famous civil and military aircraft, but developed many of the leading aero-engines of the times. Incidentally, all these road and aeronautical products carried the famous Bristol scroll insignia. A further development was the construction by BAC, since 1946, of Bristol motor cars — luxurious, hand-built sports coupes. The Bristol Aeroplane Company eventually became part of the British Aircraft Corporation, now British Aerospace. The engine division became Bristol Aero-Engines, then Bristol Siddeley, and is now part of Rolls-Royce, one of the world's three biggest aero-engine manufacturers. Sir George White was not mistaken in his decision to build aeroplanes! It meant, however, that the building of buses at Filton would have to cease, and new premises found. These were obtained on the Bath Road in Brislington, where full production was under way by 1913. Ironically, Brislington built many aircraft during the war.

Meanwhile, Bristol Tramways was extending its field of operation using motor vehicles, with over 300 taxis (mainly French-built) and about ninety assorted lorries and vans, mostly for contract work, not forgetting, of course, the hearses! All these vehicles not only worked in Bristol, but in nearby towns and cities. Motor bus or charabanc operation was established in these areas, too; Weston-super-Mare in 1910, Bath in 1911, Cheltenham in 1912 and Gloucester in 1913, although not without some opposition from local operators and businesses. Tramway systems had been built up to provide local transport in these towns; the one in Gloucester was run by the Corporation while Weston's was the least extensive, consisting of a line along the seafront, with a branch along Locking Road; this pro-

vided Bristol Tramways with more scope.

Sir George White, who had been with the firm since its outset, died in 1916. He was succeeded by his brother Samuel, who had put in over fifty years with the Company on the occasion of his own death in 1928.

Chassis production in Brislington, at the Motor Constructional Works (MCW), did not recommence after the war until 1920. The intervening years had been useful in assessing the prototype of a completely new single decker built in 1913, and this resulted in the 4 tonner of about 28—32 seats, being built from 1920. A 2 ton 20—25 seat bus was developed shortly afterwards, this being novel in having forward control, with the driver alongside the engine — many were one-man-operated. Bristol decided to offer both models for sale on the open market, and first exhibited their products at a Commercial Vehicle Exhibition in London in 1920. Their products often received glowing press reports and their position as a major manufacturer of bus chassis was thus established. Many of the bodies on the 4 tonners and 2 tonners were built by BAC, but the Company's own Body Building Works (BBW), by this time established in part of Brislington depot, produced most of the bodies on subsequent new Bristol chassis up to the mid-1930s, and even later for BT&CC's own fleet.

The Company began working services out of Swindon in 1921 (where, as at Gloucester, the Corporation provided the town's tramway network) and from Wells in 1922. The branches thus established by 1922 were to provide the Company with a basic territory, one that was to remain little changed for over sixty years. The intervening period was initially spent building a labyrinth of services, to provide rural towns and villages with a link to the larger centres. A few small operators' services were acquired as time went by. Proving more of an obstacle were the larger firms; Bath Tramways Motor Company in North-East Somerset, the National Omnibus & Transport Company in the Stroud district of Mid-Gloucestershire and the Great Western Railway's road services, operating in places like Swindon and Weston-super-Mare.

During the 1920s, some keen competition was found right on Bristol Tramways' doorstep in the form of Greyhound Motors Ltd. of Bristol. They ran several services in the city, and some to outlying points too. The competition took the usual form of racing for stops or, at best, running just ahead of the rival's buses. Greyhound also provided long-distance coach services. When the service to London was introduced, in 1925, it was the worlds first long-distance express service with scheduled boarding and alighting points en route and no pre-booking requirement. Eventually, in 1928, control of Greyhound was acquired although it was decided to retain the firm as a subsidiary, Greyhound Motors (1929) Ltd., which was periodically supplied with new stock; Bristol manufactured . . . of course!

Another small operator close to Bristol was W. J. Bence & Sons of Hanham and Longwell Green. William Bence had been in the business of building wagons since 1890 and after World War I, the firm became one of the first Ford agents in the country. Additionally, bus services were started to a variety of villages in the area, some meeting Bristol's trams at Hanham, Kingswood and Staple Hill. Then, in 1930, Bristol Tramways acquired the Bence fleet, and the depot at Hanham, once again forming a subsidiary to maintain operations, namely Bence (Motor Services) Ltd. Four new Bristol single deckers were licenced to Bence in 1930/1, two having Bence bodywork and all were registered in Gloucestershire with DG marks, in correct Bence manner.

The reduced demand for taxis resulted in the last of the famous Blue Taxis being auctioned off in 1930. The last sizeable private operator to be acquired by BT&CC, before World War II, was Burnell's Motors of Weston-super-Mare, their single deckers and coaches being taken over in 1933.

The operation of buses by the railway companies was curtailed in the late 1920s. Services and vehicles were handed over to the local bus companies but, in return, the railway companies were empowered to obtain a 50 per cent shareholding in the bus companies. The Bristol Tramways & Carriage Company, with its trams, taxis and bus building activities, was in rather a different position from the usual companies, but in 1929, the Great Western Railway was offered the shares of the late Sir George White, which were just over 50 per cent of the BT&CC shares. The GWR accepted, and its buses were absorbed in 1931. In the latter year, however, the GWR transferred its interest in BT&CC to the Western National Omnibus Company, which thereby assumed a controlling interest in Bristol Tramways. Western National itself was formed in 1929, following the GWR's acquisition of shares in the aforementioned National Omnibus & Transport Company.

This involvement by Western National, which was a member of the Tilling Group of bus operators (Thomas Tilling had once run one of London's largest bus fleets), put a Tilling representative on Bristol's Board. In 1935, the Company passed fully to Tilling control when their Chairman, J. Frederick Heaton, became Chairman of BT&CC. Henceforth, it was Tilling policy for member companies to buy Bristol chassis, normally bodied by another Tilling operator, Eastern Counties Omnibus Company or their successor, Eastern Coach Works.

The development of Bristol chassis had continued in line with changing demands and techniques. The first full-sized, forward control chassis with a reduced frame height appeared in 1925, termed the A type. Although only 23 were built, mostly with double deck bodies for municipal fleets, its design paved the way for the successful B type single decker, introduced in 1927. Some 778 Bs were built before it was eventually dropped in 1934. It was powered by a four cylinder GW petrol engine, and when Bristol's first six cylinder engine, the JW, was installed into the B type frame, the model was termed D type. Most of the fifty Ds ran for BT&CC or Greyhound.

Two experimental six-wheeled chassis, the C types, appeared in 1929, and although neither was bodied, the design was adapted for the E type trolleybus, one each being supplied to Doncaster Corporation and Pontypridd UDC. It is rumoured that one did trials on tram overhead in Central Bristol at dead of night!

In 1931, three new chassis appeared. The H type had a four cylinder LW petrol engine, while the six cylinder

The principal major bus operators neighbouring the Bristol Company, in the days before the NBC was formed, were Red & White, Midland Red, City of Oxford, Wilts & Dorset and Western National. One of the border posts was Burnham-on-Sea, where both Bristol Omnibus Company and Western National ran services to Bridgwater, but by different routes. Seen here is No. L8434 (YHT 950), one of the open platform LDs of 1956/7 intended principally for Weston-super-Mare town services. It prepares to leave on route 160, via Woolavington, while across the road, Western National FLF No. 2075 (BUO 150B) is ready to work their more direct 201 service, via Pawlett.

R. F. Mack

version, again using the JW, was termed J type. Both vehicles had a maximum length of 27ft. 6in., instead of the 26ft. length of the B and D and, as it transpired, the J was the far more widely chosen model of the two. The third chassis was the G type, which was Bristol's first chassis to be built exclusively for double deck bodywork. The operating division's first double deckers since 1909 were G types, power once again being supplied by the JW six cylinder motor.

The next few years saw considerable development. For one thing, a new four cylinder petrol engine, the NW, was introduced. After this the H type ceased production because the bearer of the new motor was termed J.NW; consequently, Js with the six cylinder JW were classified J.JW. There were a few more trial engines, but of far more significance was the installation in a J chassis, in 1933, of an oil or diesel engine. The unit was not Bristol-built, but came from Gardner's of Manchester, and had already become highly regarded since its introduction a few years before. It was a five cylinder engine (type 5LW), which proved to be the ideal combination with the Bristol chassis. Before long, production of similarly equipped JO5Gs and GO5Gs got under way, and the last petrol-engined Bristol was a J.JW coach built in 1936. Bristol's association with Gardner, established in 1933, was to last fifty years.

In the early days of using oil engines, the Motor Constructional Works installed units of several makes and power ratings, but with the introduction of the K and L in 1937, as succ sors to the G and J, the Gardner 5LW was the standard motor, the only variations being a few Ls with 4LW or 6LW units for more specific duties; for example, L4Gs were chosen to work Gloucester routes. Only after World War II was a choice of engine available again, firstly with AEC's 7.7 litre unit, then with Bristol's first mass produced oil engine, the AVW.

The reader, however, will be able to gain a picture of the development of the Bristol bus by working his way through this book. The review starts in 1936, as during that year, the Greyhound and Bence subsidiaries were absorbed, control of the neighbouring Bath companies was acquired by Bristol, the management of Gloucester Corporation Transport was taken over by Bristol, and discussions commenced with Bristol Corporation, which were to result in the formation of Bristol Joint Services in 1937.

The Tramways Act of 1870 had given Bristol Corporation the option of acquiring the Tramways Company after 21 years, or at any seven year interval thereafter. It was the Corporation's indecisive attitude that made the Company reluctant to renew or even modernise their old-fashioned open trams, knowing that once they had done so, the Corporation may buy them out. Bristol Joint Services resulted in equal representation by both parties on a committee, with the benefit of co-ordinating traffic planning and problem solving, and sharing the net revenue. The Company continued to provide the fleet, and was soon able to set about replacing the trams by buses.

Fleet Numbering

The first recognised fleet numbering system was created in 1931, when the chassis numbers of this all-Bristol fleet were applied to the bodywork in gold characters. With the arrival of the more complex chassis numbers, upon the introduction of the J.NW, JO5G, etc., some abbreviation was found necessary. For example, the former were referred to simply as N, and the latter as JOG. Eventually, in 1937, a completely new scheme was introduced, in numeric series. Petrol-engined single deckers were numbered below 1000, in various series, e.g. six cylinder Ds and Js were in the 700s, oil-engined single deckers were 2000 upwards and double deckers were 3000 upwards. The Gloucester Corporation buses 1—38 ultimately became 1201—1238, and Bath's vehicles were allocated the 800s (including their Bristols) while buses allocated to Bristol Joint Services carried a prefix C, for City.

Route Numbering

The Company's services were first numbered in 1913; the numbers 1—17 were allocated for the tram services (they later became disused), while bus routes became 18 upwards, commencing with the Suspension Bridge route. The services running in 1936 were not numbered in any strict groups, although there were several sequential numbers in many areas. For example, Weston-super-Mare's routes were numbered in the lower regions of the 40s, 90s, 150s and 160s, routes out of Cheltenham were numbered 45—49, 61—64 and 170—173, those out of Gloucester included 50—60 and 107—120, the Forest of Dean routes were 100—106 and 121—122 while Swindon area routes were 65—77 and 180—184. Bristol City and Country routes were somewhat intermingled, in various ranges.

Suffix letters were used to denote variations to the main service, although on Bristol City routes, a further method was the addition of a 200 prefix, resulting in pairs like 36/236, 84/284 and 132/232. One known use on Country services was for the link between the ends of services 136 and 137, which was 237 (Frome to Shepton Mallet). On the abandonment of Bristol's trams, from 1938, the replacement bus routes were numbered 1 to 9 in order of introduction.

The services of the Bath companies were numbered in their own series, Bath city routes being 1 to 20 and their country routes upwards from 36. Gloucester city services also had their own series from 1 and, furthermore, Cheltenham District services (acquired in 1950) were numbered from 1! The routes in the Hanham area, based on Bence's network, were numbered 300 upwards by BT&CC, while ex-Western National routes at Stroud were renumbered into the 400s.

During the 1960s, moves were made to bring Bristol City route numbers below 100 as chances arose, normally following service revisions. For example, the 133 and 144 absorbed the 7 and became the 13 and 14. Another plan saw the removal of suffix letters by giving the affected routes a number adjacent to the main service, even if it required renumbering, for example 2/2A became 22/23 (the old 22 had to become 42) while 84/84B became 84/85.

In 1966 and 1967, all the Company's routes, excepting City services, were renumbered into regional series, in the following progression:-

100s	Weston town, Weston and Wells country, southern Bath country;
200s	Bath city, remaining Bath country, (taking care not to duplicate Western National's Wiltshire routes);
300s	Bristol Country, Hanham locals;
400s	Stroud and Swindon areas;
500s	Gloucester city, Gloucester and Cheltenham country, Cheltenham town

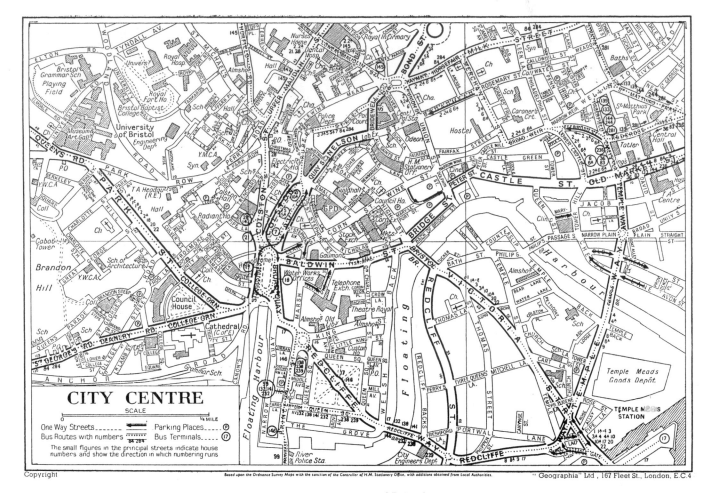

Map of the City of Bristol.

Extract from 1945 Timetable.

| Light hour figures denote A.M. | | | | | | | | | | | Heavy hour figures denote P.M. |

BATH 63 — FROME — CHAPMANSLADE — DEAD MAIDS — BATH 63

Mondays, Wednesdays and Saturdays

					SO	Through Fares							SO	Through Fares
						Single	Return							Single	Return
Frome, Market Place	9 48	2 7	6 7	8 45				Dead Maids	10 5	2 23	6 23	9 5		
Chapmanslade	10 0	2 19	6 19	8 57		5d.	9d.	C apmans ade	10 8	2 26	5 26	9 8		—	—
Dead Maids	10 3	2 22	6 22	9 0		6d.	10d.	Frome, Market Place	1020	2 3c	6 38	9 20		6d.	10d.

SO—Saturdays only.

BATH 64 — FROME — MELLS — RADSTOCK — BATH 64

	Weekdays			Sundays	Through Fares			Weekdays			Sundays	Through Fares	
					Single	Return						Single	Return
Frome, Market Place	1020	2 20	6 20	4 20			Radstock, Station	1130	3 30	7 40	1 30	5 40		
Great Elm	1029	2 29	6 29	4 29	4d.	—	Westfield	1134	3 34	7 44	1 34	5 44	2d.	—
Mells	1034	2 34	6 34	4 34	5d.	—	Stratton-on-the-Fosse	1142	3 42	7 52	1 42	5 52	5d.	—
Vobster	1039	2 39	6 39	4 39	6d.	—	Highbury	1154	3 54	8 4	1 54	6 4	9d.	—
Highbury	1044	2 44	6 44	4 44	7d.	—	Vobster	1159	3 59	8 9	1 59	6 9	1/-	—
Stratton-on-the-Fosse	1056	2 56	6 56	4 56	10d.	—	Mells	12 4	4 4	8 14	2 4	6 14	1/1	—
Westfield	11 4	3 4	7 4	5 4	1/1	—	Great Elm	12 9	4 9	8 19	2 9	6 19	1/2	—
Radstock, Station	11 8	3 8	7 8	5 8	1/3	—	Frome, Market Place	1218	4 18	8 28	2 18	6 28	1/3	—

Plate 1: The mainstay of the Bristol Tramways motor bus fleet in 1936 was the Bristol B type. Nearly 300 of these sucessful 30 to 32 seat single deckers were supplied between 1927 and 1934, their styling changing as the fashion changed. One of the earlier examples, No. 371 (HW 8366), is seen here at the 'Tramways Centre' circa 1937 (during the building of Electricity House), while on layover from the long Bristol to Cheltenham route 29. A new J type stands across the road, working service 88 to Radstock. The buses carry the handsome dark blue and white livery, with the Bristol coat of arms on the sides.

George Vowles

Plate 2: When control of Bath Electric Tramways Ltd. and Bath Tramways Motor Company Ltd. was taken up by Bristol Tramways, the fleet contained a very mixed selection of new and second-hand single deckers. There were several AECs and ADCs, however, and even a few Bristol A types. In this view of a number of the white-roofed green buses at Parade Gardens, a 1931 AEC Regal with Park Royal B30F bodywork, FB 9224, passes a line of vehicles headed by one of the six 1928 AEC 426 models, with Harrington B32D bodies, acquired from Timpson's of Hastings. In the distance, a tram can be seen rounding Orange Grove.

Bristol Vintage Bus Group Collection

Plate 3: A family concern, W. J. Bence & Sons, operated bus services in the Hanham, Kingswood and Longwell Green region, to the east of Bristol. The business was acquired by Bristol Tramways in 1930, although the fleet remained as a subsidiary until 1936, after which it was absorbed into the Bristol fleet. The Bence stock contained several small buses based, for example, on Ford, Star Flyer and Reo chassis, although there were AECs and Daimlers too. The bodywork was built at their Longwell Green Factory which, under the later name of Longwell Green Coachworks, remained in existence until 1983. This Daimler, carrying Bence's green livery, was retired long before Bristol Tramways absorbed the fleet.

Bristol Vintage Bus Group

Plate 4: Since becoming a subsidiary in 1928, Greyhound Motors had been supplied with plenty of new Bristol buses and coaches. These included three G type double deckers, delivered in 1931/2 for their Bristol City routes, including service 84 to Downend and service 99 to Avonmouth via The Portway. HY 6198, seen here in Prince Street on route 99, had stylish Beadle bodywork painted in the grey and white livery. Greyhound was fully absorbed on 1st January 1936, although the fleet-name was retained for coach services. In 1937, this bus was numbered C3002 in the Tramways fleet, carrying another two bodies before the chassis was sold in 1955.

Allan Macfarlane Collection

Plate 5: The all single decker fleet of 38 Gloucester Corporation buses was based on Thornycroft and Vulcan chassis, many being designed to normal control layout. All Vulcans were sold by Tramways by 1941, but the Thornycrofts kept going until the post-war years, with the newest receiving Gardner 4LW motors in 1945. This view of No. 33 (FH 8291), which BT&CC renumbered 1233, shows the unusual open rear platform arrangement of its locally-built Gloucester Railway Carriage & Wagon Company body. It is a 1933 Thornycroft BC 32 seater, and it carries the Corporation's crimson lake livery.

Elvin J. Young Collection

Plate 6: From 1937, Bristol Tramways began to re-equip the various 'subsidiary' fleets with new vehicles which, naturally, were of Bristol manufacture. As exemplified by the first Gloucester Bristol, No. 1240 (the number 1239 was not used), these buses were registered in the appropriate cities,.this one being BFH 502. Although painted in Tramways' dark blue and white livery, it carried the Gloucester coat of arms on the sides. No. 1240 was a Bristol B34D-bodied JO, powered by a four cylinder Dennis engine which was deemed sufficient for Gloucester's flat terrain; the Dennis engines fitted in Nos. 1240—5, were replaced by four cylinder Gardners in 1947. The bus is seen here, some way from home, at Weston-super-Mare, and is about to be passed by No. 3041 (CHY 118), a 1936 GO5G, on town service 152.

George Vowles

Plate 7: Bath Tramways had probably been responsible for the order for twenty more AEC Regal chassis, before Bristol Tramways took control in December 1936. However, the body contract showed some 'Tilling' influence, in favouring Eastern Coach Works, but an ECW order was surprising, as BT&CC usually supplied its needs from its own Body Building Works. Furthermore, their styling was intriguing; the only ECW bodies they resembled were those built for West Yorkshire on Bristol JO5G and L5G chassis, even down to the 'bible board' destination indicators. Whereas the latter were forward entrance, Bath's had rear entrances. In common with the Gloucester Division, Bristol's blue and white livery was carried by these AECs, but with the belted BATH fleetname. No. 2226 (GL 5077 — registered in Bath, of course) and a twin, stand here at Parade Gardens.

Bristol Vintage Bus Group Collection

Plate 8: Fourteen J type coaches were delivered to BT&CC in 1937, and took the numbers 2201—2214 (DHY 653—666) before the 2200s were reserved for Bath saloons to use. The coach bodies were to a restrained but pleasant design by Duple; this being another new supplier to the Company. Nos. 2201—6 were rare JO6A models, with AEC 7.7 litre engines, the others being JO5Gs. No. 2203 displays the pre-war coach livery of blue with white trim, and the Bristol coat of arms was also carried by coaches at this time.

Michael J. Tozer Collection

Plate 9: Duple also supplied the 26 seat bodywork on six Dennis Maces, delivered in 1937. These attractive little buses, with their overhanging noses, spent a lifetime bouncing around Weston-super-Mare until 1954/5. No. 654 (DHY 650), in typical post-war guise, rests in Weston bus station between duties on the Sand Bay route.

Mike Mogridge

Plate 10: The crimson trams of the Weston-super-Mare District Electric Supply Company Ltd. finally fell to the blue buses of the Bristol Tramways in April 1937, after lengthy competition. Some new GO5Gs were added to the town's existing Gs that summer *(see Plate 6)*, including No. 3077 (EAE 286). The bodies featured a more severe frontal slope than hitherto, together with the new larger destination boxes. It is believed they were the last buses to have the destination blind winding handles placed outside, the Bristol Company being unusual in placing the handles in the cab on subsequent buses.

George Vowles

Plate 16: Single deckers continued to be added to the Company's fleets over the same period; for example, two dozen L5G saloons were allocated to Bath Tramways where they brought about considerable standardisation to that section, leaving just a handful of 1930—4 AEC Regals from the original company's stock. Seen here at Grand Parade, ready to leave for Bradford-on-Avon, is No. 2256 (GL 6621), a 1939 bus with B32F bodywork. A route number stencil would normally be carried in the top box. Gloucester City's new Ls of the period, incidentally, were powered by Gardner 4LW engines; Eastern Counties was the only other company to run L4Gs.

George Vowles

Plate 17: A revised style of Duple coach body, with forward entrance, was supplied on fourteen L5Gs in 1939 (Nos. 2143—56: FHT 290, FHT 781—793). They carried a reversed livery of white with blue relief and displayed a modernised 'Greyhound and Hoop' motif, and a small Bristol scroll was placed on the emergency door, opposite the entrance door. No. 2144 is seen here early in the war years, awaiting its turn on the Southsea express service. Enemy action resulted in Nos. 2155 and 2156 receiving utility bus bodies, but Nos. 2143—54 returned to coaching duties after the war until their 1952 retirement.

George Vowles

Plate 18: Seven Bedford WTBs, again with Duple bodywork, entered service in 1939 (FHT 817—23). They commenced a new lightweight vehicle numbering series, Nos. 200—206. No. 200 had 'Vista' coach bodywork, but the others had 'Luton' bus bodies. No. 200 is seen here, with its proud driver, after receiving British European Airways colours in 1948. The seven were withdrawn in 1950, when many new Bedford-Duples entered service.

Michael Mogridge

Plate 19: The opportunity was taken, in 1939, to try a demonstration model AEC Regent in service in Bristol. The bus, JML 784, had bodywork by Weymann and is seen here on the Downs, accompanied by the contemporary ECW-bodied K5G No. C3120 (EHY 582).

S. Miles Davey

Plate 20: The end of Bath's trams came between October 1938 and May 1939. To replace the bulk of them, Bath Electric Tramways Ltd. received thirty Bristol double deckers with 5LW engines, and the latest BBW bodywork. Fourteen of these, (Nos. 3800—3813 : GL 6601—14) were K5Gs, but Nos. 3814—3829 were rather interesting GO5Gs. Their 1936 chassis had originally been supplied to Maidstone & District and Chatham & District, with Weymann bodies, and they were registered DKN 31—46. In 1938, the chassis were returned to Bristol in part-exchange for new K5Gs, which were given the Weymann bodies, the DKNs then receiving new Bristol bodies for the Bath fleet. No. 3814 (DKN 31) is seen on the Guildhall and Twerton route, at the Bath Abbey stop. The belt surrounding the Bath fleetname contains Bath Tramways Motor Company's name! Note the wheel nut guard ring.

Peter Hulin Collection

Plate 21: With the coming of World War II, in September 1939, munitions factories and Army camps sprang up all over the place, and put pressure on the local bus companies to provide transport for construction workers. Wilts & Dorset was under particular pressure, because of the Salisbury Plain camps, so they bought hoards of elderley double deckers, mainly Leylands. When the pressure eased, as building neared completion, the buses were sold and BT&CC took the opportunity to buy several. Some were placed in the Gloucester city fleet, jointly with some ex-North Western TD1s, and being their first double deckers, they were numbered 1500—1504. The rest became Country services Nos. 3610—9 (with so many City buses on order, from No. C3082, additional Country buses started a new series at 3600). Seen here, after the war, is No. L3615 (CM 8725), a 1929 TD1 from Birkenhead Corporation. The body, however, came from Cardiff Corporation and is a 1932 Northern Counties product, fitted by Tramways. The bus was one of several loaned to Crosville during 1948/9 (working not a million miles from Birkenhead!), with many later being purchased by Crosville.

Allan Macfarlane Collection

Plate 22: As the pressures of war grew, so restrictions had to be imposed to enable the best use to be made of available materials. Bus body construction took on a severe, square-cornered look, while the styling and finish that one was used to in peacetime disappeared, to be replaced by single-skin panelling, hard seats, reduced ventilation and poor lighting. Also gone was the dignified blue and white livery — for ever! New buses arrived in a grim khaki, while the existing fleet donned a coat of grey over the white paint, to make the buses less conspicuous from the air. It was, however, 1942 before the war had the most pronounced effect on buses. In the previous year, Bristol's Motor Constructional Works, together with all other chassis builders, had been ordered to stop chassis production but, after a while, some, including Bristol, were permitted to complete chassis for which parts were in stock. These were known as 'Unfrozen' chassis, and the Bristols made up the builder's 56th Sanction of 17 Ls and 57th Sanction of 87 Ks. Most of the Unfrozen Ks taken into the Bristol fleet had Bristol utility bodies, built to a very distinctive design, being derived from the pre-war body, with the six bays and rather small windows. No. 3628 (HHU 351) was the first to enter service in khaki livery, and is seen on Bristol's Centre. Incidentally, upon the outbreak of war, the abandonment of Bristol's trams was discontinued, leaving the routes to Kingswood and Hanham and to Bedminster Down and Ashton. Enemy action, however, sealed their fate in 1941 with the bombing of Bedminster tram depot, and St. Philips Bridge and the power cables from the adjacent power-station, on Good Friday, 1941.

Peter Hulin

Plate 23: After the Unfrozen chassis had been completed, only Guy and Daimler were authorised to build double deck chassis. Bristol received a modest allocation of twelve Guy Arabs, complete with the familiar Gardner 5LW engine, carrying bodies by Park Royal or, in the case of the final bus, by Weymann. These were to full utility specification, with only one opening window on each side of each saloon, an unglazed rear upper deck emergency window and, probably, spring-filled leather seats. They were placed in service during 1942/3 and spent their entire lives at Weston-super-Mare, where No. 3635 (HHU 357) was photographed outside the railway station.

S. L. Poole,
Courtesy London Bus Preservation Group Ltd.

Plate 24: In contrast to the small Guy allocation, BT&CC received no fewer than fifty Bedford OWBs. They were divided almost equally between City and Country services (Nos. C231—C257 and 258—280), and they had the added discomfort of wooden slatted seats. With their spitting carburettors and the shrill ring to their gearboxes, there was no mistaking these buses while they served the Tramways. They were withdrawn during 1950/1, after a relatively short career. Seen here is No. C231 (HHU 299), when new.

Allan Macfarlane Collection

Plate 25: During the war, the Company decided that several of their surplus coaches, principally B types and, surprisingly, 1935 32 seat Js, should be given new bus bodies. These were built to the Ministry of Supply utility specification, with much of the construction being undertaken by Bence at Longwell Green. The bus operating business of W. J. Bence & Sons had, of course, been acquired in 1930, and remained a subsidiary until 1936. The bodyworks continued under the Bence name until the closing years of the war, when Longwell Green Coach Works was formed. Bence-rebodied 1929 B type No. 587 (HW 6636), which carried 28 seats around the perimeter of the saloon, is seen here, after setting down 'Charlie Chaplin' outside Hanham depot! Note Bert Bence's garage across the road; Bert was one of William's sons.

George Vowles

Plate 26: The pre-war coach livery was primarily blue *(see Plates 8, 11, and 12)* and, consequently, the wartime application of grey was less extensive. No. 745 (AHW 534), a 1934 petrol-engined J 26 seat coach, is seen here seconded to a bus service to the aircraft works, and displays a shockingly bald front tyre! No. 745 was one of about 39 single deckers and three double deckers that ran on gas during the war, most being Ds or Js with six cylinder petrol engines. A few, including the new L6GGs Nos. 2169 and 2170 (HHT 459 and HHT 460), and G type No. C3002 (HY 6198), *see Plate 4,* had the gas unit built into the body, but the general method was to tow a gas-producing trailer.

S. L. Poole,
Courtesy London Bus Preservation Group Ltd.

Plate 27: One of the 1935 Js with a well-rounded B32F body, No. 2119 (BHW 433), is seen here, in wartime colours, with fresh white paint having been applied to the front wings and, wisely, the entrance steps. This bus was one of several that originally had been powered by a four cylinder NW petrol engine. BT&CC had commenced a programme of replacing the petrol engines in all Gs, Hs and Js in 1937, breaking off in 1940 for the duration of the war (apart from an isolated example) and completing the conversions between 1945 and 1949. No. 2119 had received its 5LW in 1939 and accordingly, it was renumbered from 616. It will be noticed that new and modernised single deckers were completely intermingled in the 2000 series.

Peter Hulin

Plate 28: The white wing tips really show up well against the dull blue and grey on this 1935 G. Like No. 2119, it was equipped with a 5LW, in 1939, in place of its petrol engine, but was one of several buses, including all Gs and fifty Js, to be numbered in the 'oil-engined series' in the 1937 scheme, in preparation for the change of engine. No. 3014 (BHY 694) stands in Marlborough before returning to Swindon, in 1943.

S. L. Poole,
Courtesy London Bus Preservation Group Ltd.

Plate 29: One of the worst attrocities of the war was an unexpected daylight air raid on the Broad Weir area of Central Bristol, during a morning rush-hour in August 1942. Three fully laden K5Gs, No. C3102 (EHY 564), No. C3262 (GAE 460) and No. C3352 (GHU 489) were caught in the blast which caused an awful loss of life, the buses becoming twisted wrecks. Despite that, the chassis were salvaged and, a year later, returned to service with new utility bodies by Brush of Loughborough; a manufacturer seldom featured in the Tramways fleet. No. C3352 is seen here, after the war, on route 4A. It was withdrawn in 1950, and its subsequent history will be found in *Plate 69*.

Bristol Vintage Bus Group Collection

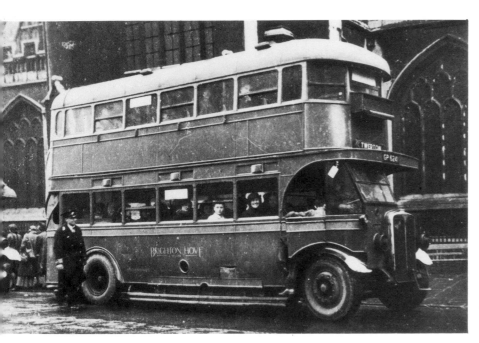

Plate 30: Numerous buses of all manner of makes and types were hired during the war, some for quite long spells. Some Bristols were available for borrowing, but Tramways had to get used to many unfamiliar types. A Brighton, Hove & District AEC Regent, with Tilling outside staircase body, is seen here beside Bath Abbey, accompanied by a Bath Tramways AEC Regal.

S. L. Poole,
Courtesy London Bus Preservation Group Ltd.

Plate 31: Things began to brighten up in 1945, not only politcally, but also in the bus fleet. A brand-new livery made its appearance on the Company's buses; Tilling Green, relieved by two cream bands. At first, the lower band was applied beneath the lower deck windows, as seen here on one of the first buses repainted green, 1941 K5G No. C3335 (GHT 153). In the early post-war years, most pre-war buses had their front registration plates removed from the radiator, and painted on to the front dash instead.

Peter Hulin Collection

Plate 32: Despite the note of optimism, new buses continued to be delivered to the Ministry of Supply's utility specification, although the Motor Constructional Works was one of the privileged few empowered to recommence chassis building, in 1944. The works concentrated initially on Ks, now powered by six cylinder AEC 7.7 engines, with which, of course, they were familiar. The first batch entered Tramways' service during 1944/5, as Nos. 3642—55 (HHY 586—99); interestingly, their bodies were of lowbridge layout, being the first such double deckers delivered new. Construction was undertaken by Strachan. No. 3646 onwards arrived in green livery, but No. 3651, seen here, shows a slightly later development, with a prefix letter L to denote lowbridge bus.

Michael J. Tozer

Plate 33: The City fleet had not received any new double deckers since 1941, so it was glad to receive a consignment of utility K6As in 1945. The first five, Nos. C3354—8 (JAE 126—30), had Park Royal bodies, similar to, but less austere than, those carried by the Guy Arabs *(see Plate 23)*. Exemplifying this batch is No. C3358, seen on lay-over from route 142. Nos. C3359—73 (JAE 251—65, the last was a K5G), had very attractively proportioned Duple bodies, while Nos. LC3374—8 (JAE 762—6) of 1946, carried low-bridge Strachan bodies, as shown in *Plate 32*.

Michael Mogridge

Plate 34: The City's final utility Ks, Nos. C3379—84 (JHT 18—23) all of which had the new, so called, PV2 low radiator (introduced by No. LC3377), had a claim to fame in that they were the only Bristol K chassis to carry highbridge Strachan bodies. No. C3384 is shown, in the 1950s, at the Carey's Lane, Old Market, terminus of the circuitous route 83 to the Suspension Bridge.

Geoff. Gould, Courtesy Bristol Vintage Bus Group

Plate 35: Further Duple-bodied Ks were added to the Country and Bath Tramways fleets in 1946, the latter introducing a new fleetname of Bath Services. Seen here when brand-new is Country bus No. 3671 (JHT 120), the fourth bus of a batch of fourteen.

S. Miles Davey

Plate 36 (above): An early indication that things were returning to normal came with the arrival, in 1946, of new Ks and Ls, with bodies built to peacetime standards (if not materials). Their bodies were made by ECW, to the completely new designs introduced by this firm following prototypes built during the war. Bristol's own Body Building Works became heavily involved in building new bodies for older chassis from 1946. The first post-war ECW bodies featured square-cornered sliding vents above rounded fixed glazing, as exemplified by the new No. 2173 (JHT 826). Note also the completely new destination indicator; somewhat bigger than previous specimens, it had a shallow top aperture and larger lower section, in which it resembled the new screen adopted by other Tilling fleets. This layout, however, did not find favour with Tramways, who subsequently evolved a single screen measuring 36in. x 18in. No. 2173 carries temporary paper displays, listing both terminal points.

Peter Hulin

Plate 37: The first post-war City Ks also had the square-vented windows and two piece destination screens but, as with the Ls, these screens were modified to the large single display. No. C3394 (JHT 810) is seen here on 29th November 1953, the first day that route 8 was extended to Hartcliffe (Hareclive Road) during the building of the vast housing estate — although, from the background, that is difficult to believe!

Gordon Richmond

Plate 38: In April 1946, Bristol Tramways commenced what was to be their five year rebodying programme, in which all Gs, the one surviving H, virtually all Js (other than those rebodied during the war), plus a few early Ks and Ls were fitted with new bodies. The first buses to be treated were five 1936 Country GO5Gs, which received new lowbridge bodies, and were completed by Longwell Green Coach Works; they even carried Longwell Green transfers on the sides! *(see Plate 25).* These new bodies were somewhat pre-war in appearance. In 1948, the five were transferred to Gloucester as Nos. L1515—9, No. L1515 being seen here at Cheltenham. While at Gloucester they received low PV2 radiators. In 1951, they moved on to Bath Services as Nos. L3906—10 and whilst here, were equipped with AEC 7.7 litre engines. They returned to Country services in 1952, this time numbered L4151/0/2—4! They were retired, exhausted, in 1955.

Michael J. Tozer

Plate 39: The bodies displaced from the GO5Gs, in 1946, by the new lowbridge bodies, shown in *Plate 38*, were too good to waste. Therefore they were remounted on the oldest five Gs in the fleet, Nos. C3000—4 of 1931/2, replacing Bristol, Brush, Beadle and Cowieson bodies of typical early 1930s appearance *(see Plate 4)*. Seen here with the body from No. 3040 (CHY 117) is the first G type, No. C3000 (HY 3630, chassis G101), which had received its 5LW engine only three months previously. This rebodying was only a temporary measure, as all five were fitted with new bodies during 1948—1950 *(see Plate 54)*.

Michael Mogridge

Plate 40: In the early post-war years, BT&CC acquired some more elderly Leyland Titans and AEC Regents. They came from Plymouth and Exeter Corporations and, additionally, Exeter Corporation made available their five Bristol GO5Gs. One of these (AHW 953) had been built as a demonstrator, with a Weymann body and, experimentally, a Beardmore engine (a GO6B at the time), although it later received a 5LW. The others were Bristol-bodied 1935 buses, which presented a familiar appearance. However, they featured a straight staircase, resulting in a full-width seat across the back of the upper deck, and the peculiar lower deck window layout, discernible in this view of No. 3665 (BFJ 157) at Cheltenham.

Colin Martin Collection

Plate 41: With an eye open for a bargain, BT&CC was one of several operators, both large and small, to buy ten year old ECW saloon bodies from North Western Road Car Company in 1946. These bodies, originally mounted on JO5G chassis, were distinctly North Western in styling, with their half-canopies and single piece windscreens *(see Plate 7)*. One of these bodies is seen here mounted on No. 2366 (AHW 539), a 1934 J that had originally looked like AHW 534 featured in *Plate 26*. All those AHU/AHW coaches received second-hand saloon bodies during the war (excluding the requisitioned AHU 808), then were renumbered 2350—66 on receiving 5LWs during 1945/7. All received new bodies by 1951 *(see Plate 57)*.

Allan Macfarlane Collection

Plate 42: In 1947, the City fleet was equipped with twenty new L5Gs, Nos. C2711—30 (JHT 846—65). In order to match the other City single deckers, their ECW bodies were of dual-doorway layout, a pattern that was evolved exclusively for BT&CC. The way in which the front door was neatly incorporated into the standard ECW body is shown here by No. C2726, pictured leaving the Redcliffe swing bridge, close to its City terminus. When the buses were quite new, the front door was converted to electric control and was operated by the driver.

Michael Mogridge

Plate 43: In 1947 the Tilling Group, which was shortly to be nationalised as part of the British Transport Commission, ordered 100 Leyland PD1A Titans, with lowbridge ECW bodies, for distribution to member fleets. In addition, fifty PD1s were allocated to BT&CC, of which 25 were to have highbridge ECW bodies, the other 25 receiving H56R bodies in Tramways' own body shops — some of the few new chassis to go through BBW after the war, none of which were Bristols! These Titans were placed in the City fleet, as Nos. C4000—49, and spent most of their lives at Eastville depot. No. C4001 (KHW 242) poses outside the depot when new, and displays the rather severe lines of the 1947—50 Bristol body, together with economy destination blinds. Their radiators were a mixture of black-painted metal and chrome.

Bristol Vintage Bus Group

Plate 44: The programme of building new Bristol B35R bodies for the 1933—7 J chassis got off to a flying start during 1946—8, with over forty being treated. Generally, the oldest chassis were dealt with first, all having previously received 5LW engines in place of their petrol units. Initially, the chassis retained their high radiators, as exhibited here by No. 2014 (HY 8257), but before long all were re-equipped with PV2 radiators. No. 2014 of 1933 bears a 1948 body with round-cornered vents, and is seen in Bristol's Haymarket, where there is evidence that horse-drawn transport still had its place in the world.

Michael Mogridge

Plate 45 (below): It was 1948 before the coach fleet was able to be updated. New that year were twelve L6Bs with 31 seat coach versions of the ECW body. These handsome vehicles featured polished brightwork, a green flash on the cream side panels, extra panelling down to the guard rails and an extra sliding ventilator in the first nearside bay. No. 2378 (KHW 643) stands in Prince Street, Bristol, beneath the canopy of the waiting-room and cafe. As early as 1954, all twelve coaches had been reseated to B35R, and painted in bus livery.

Michael Mogridge

Plate 46: Early in 1948, the Gloucester city fleet was given its first Bristol double deckers in the form of ten new or nearly new K5Gs, K6As and K6Bs numbered 1505—14. No. 1508 (KHU 618), a K6A, had entered service late in 1947 as Country services bus No. 3696, but was one of six transferred to Gloucester in January 1948. This bus and twin, No. 1510, were fitted with replacement bodies ten years later *(see Plate 127)*, so lasting until 1965 — their contemporaries were despatched during 1959—61. Note the Gloucester coat of arms on the side.

Peter Davey

Plate 47: The first new lowbridge buses since the war appeared during 1947/8, and started two new numbering series. The Bath Services buses were numbered L3900 onwards, while the Country service examples became L4100 et seq (the L prefix was not always carried at first). No. L3905 (KHU 606) proceeds at speed along the then tree-lined Pultney Street, Bath, with blinds set for its return trip to Trowbridge. The first nine months of life for this K6A were spent as Country bus No. L4109. After withdrawal as early as 1959, this bus saw further service with Thames Valley.

P. R. Forsey

Plate 48: The most prolific post-war year for the intake of new stock was 1948, as close on 180 new vehicles were received, not to mention new bodies on old chassis! The most numerous variant was the Country highbridge K, of which over sixty examples entered service, most bearing LAE registrations. No. 3758 (LAE 719) was one of the last buses to come with wood-framed ECW bodywork, many of which were rebuilt by ECW ten years later or, failing that, were withdrawn in the early 1960s. The bus is seen working City route 232; there was always a small presence of Country buses on City work (known as B fleet duties) in order to balance mileage covered by City buses working outside the boundary, especially on works and schools duties.

Allan Macfarlane Collection

Plate 49: Buses delivered from the end of 1948 — the LHUs — introduced an improved ECW body utilising metal framework. Although externally there was little difference, the interior finish had a less bulky structure. A chassis modification introduced about the same time (with the 68th K Sanction and 71st L Sanction), saw the fitting of a flush side-light on the dash, causing the registration plate and fleet number to swap positions. No. C3424 (LHU 531) had its capacity increased experimentally to H31/28R, by using the lowbridge K's lower deck layout and replacing one of the stairhead single seats by a double. This useful arrangement became standard from LHU 987 but, surprisingly, was copied by no other operator. The first 59 seat buses were Nos. 3765—72, and No. 3772 (LHU 994) is seen here. Compare the wheel arch seat with that in *Plate 48*. Shortly these buses became Bath Services Nos. 3865—72, together with 56 seater No. 3864 (ex-3764), displaying a lazy method of renumbering.

Michael Mogridge

Plate 50:   Bath Services received a sizeable fleet of new Ls after the war, a typical example being No. 2284 (LHW 907), a 1949 L5G. The Bath Services fleetname shows up well on this bus, which was photographed at Parade Gardens on cross-city route 10. Despite its metal-framed body, No. 2284 was withdrawn in 1960, although, with another body, it served as stores van No. W96 until 1965.

Allan Macfarlane Collection

Plate 51:   Twelve very unusual single deckers entered service in 1949. They had new L5G chassis, but these had been supplied for use only in rebuilding or replacing worn out stock — their chassis numbers had an R suffix. Similar chassis went to Eastern Counties and United Auto. Bristol's rebuilding consisted of taking out of service twelve circa 1930 B types, which carried 1943/4 Bence bodies — the bodies were then removed, rebuilt and lengthened (amidships), and were then fitted to the L5Gs. To prove that Bs had been replaced, not only were the B type chassis numbers reissued, now with a suffix L (they did not display their 73rd Sanction numbers), but the circa 1930 registrations were transferred! Bath received Nos. 2296—9 (HW 8369, HW 9059, HW 8370 and HW 9493) and Country services took Nos. 2420—7 (DG 1432, HW 9499 and 9576, HY 1956, HY 1953, HY 2398, HY 2394 and HY 2396) of which No. 2420 is seen here at Swindon. Coincidentally the B with this Gloucester registration was supplied new to Bence of Hanham *(see Plate 3)*.

Michael J. Tozer

Plate 52:   ECW built an experimental batch of four bay Ks in 1949, with single examples being supplied to Brighton, Bristol and York-West Yorkshire, while Eastern Counties had several. Bristol's was No. C3436 (LHY 925), the first of the 1949/50 delivery of buses featuring what were known as 'thin-wall' bodies of a very much smoother interior finish, in which the windows were set flush with the interior panels. This was to remain ECW's standard until 1981! Very comfortable seats of London Transport's pattern were installed, but totalling only 56 in No. C3436 instead of the new standard of 59.

Michael J. Tozer

Plate 53:   Another most interesting delivery in 1949 was the prototype Bristol Lodekka, a design which had the overall height of a lowbridge bus, yet featured the central upper deck gangway of the highbridge bus. To achieve this, the chassis was redesigned to reduce the height of the lower saloon floor, therefore eliminating the step from the platform; this caused some humerous reactions from people who weren't looking where they were stepping! Numbered C5000 (LHY 949), it demonstrated to other B.T.C. fleets before settling down to work City lowbridge route 36. It is seen here, arriving in Carey's Lane, Old Market (today, the Inner Ring Road and the Holiday Inn would form the backdrop) and can be compared with a standard K. Later known as No. LC5000, the bus was scrapped in 1963.

Michael Mogridge

Plate 54:   The policy of new bodies for old chassis returned to double deckers in 1948 *(see Plate 38)*. Five Gs were put through BBW that year, and between late 1948 and mid-1950 all untreated Gs, nearly 100 of them, received PV2 radiators and went to ECW for new H56R or H59R bodies, as shown by Country bus No. 3076 (EAE 597). The placing of the gearbox amidships caused a high floor level, which resulted in the large square windscreen and the first bay was shortened slightly, hence the lack of a ventilator upstairs.

Peter Davey

Plate 55:   Bath had a large proportion of these rebodied Gs, having the sixteen ex-Maidstone & District buses, Nos. 3814—29, in their midst *(see Plate 20)*. No. 3819 (DKN 36) stands outside Bath Spa Station on service 19, a route which frequently employed the buses.

R. H. G. Simpson

Plate 56: In 1949, as all Gs were committed to rebodying, the Tramways turned its attention to the pre-war Ks. Several 1938/9 examples were treated by BBW, but two oddities were Nos. C3096 and C3098 (EHY 558 and EHY 560) which received new bodies manufactured by Welsh Metal Industries of Caerphilly. These were instantly recognisable by their well-rounded rear domes. No. C3096 is seen in Crow Lane, Henbury, a scene that remains little altered today — *(see Plate 241).*
Michael Mogridge

Plate 57: Single deck rebodying charged ahead also, but took two new directions in 1949. Firstly, in addition to the Js, some pre-war Ls went through BBW and, secondly, 28 Js were sent to ECW for new B35R bodies. The high positioning of the 5LW in the J, however, caused the fire wall between the engine and cab to be higher, resulting in a shallower cab nearside window and a marginally shallower windscreen. These are discernible in this view of No. 2363 (AHW 536) pictured at Swindon. The last thirteen of these bodies dispensed with the side destination box and carried an extra sliding ventilator there; new Ls followed suit in 1950.
Michael Mogridge

Plate 58: Appropriately, the last petrol-engined Bristol to be built, J.JW226, was the last to be re-equipped with a 5LW, although this did not occur until 1949. The vehicle, now renumbered from 762 to 2367 (CHW 567) carried the last of three Bristol luxury coach bodies to be constructed in 1935/6. Used as an ambulance during the war, the coach was back on its intended duties, in this view, in Queen Square, Bristol. The young man on the bicycle was responsible for several of the photographs used in this book — it's Mike Mogridge!
Michael J. Tozer

Plate 59: A new fleet of lightweight, small capacity single deckers — petrol engined at that — appeared during 1949/50 in the form of Bedford OBs with, perhaps predictably, Duple B30F bodies. These were particularly associated with Weston-super-Mare but, at times, also ran at Bristol, Gloucester and Stroud. In later days, some exchanged engines with Perkins diesels from Hants & Dorset OBs. These served Tramways for up to twelve years and included No. 217 (MHU 59) which is seen when new at Weston's Grand Pier stop. Note the London-style Johnson typeface used for the route number!

S. N. J. White

Plate 60: Eight Duple Vista coach-bodied OBs also joined BT&CC in 1950, but these were much shorter-lived, all being sold in 1955. No. 226 (MHU 998) is seen arriving at London's Victoria Coach Station.

R. F. Mack

Plate 61: Many B.T.C. fleets placed small numbers of Beadle chassisless buses in service around 1949/50 and BT&CC was no exception. Their two examples, Nos. 2500 and 2501 (MHU 246 and MHU 247) used Morris Commercial running units and Saurer oil engines. The buses were of an experimental nature, and were retired in 1958.

Michael Mogridge

Plate 62:   Following the twenty dual-door Ls of 1947 *(see Plate 42)*, the City placed in service a further 29 during 1949/50 (Nos. C2732—60: LHY 972—989, MHW 977—987). These were of the latest specification, however, with 'thin-wall' bodies and London-style seats. The L5Gs among them (Nos. C2737—44 and C2750—2 were L6Bs) also featured flexible engine mountings, which appreciably reduced the noise internally. Country services B35R versions, Nos. 2442—5 and 2447—64 (LHY 990—999 and MHW 988—999) were to the same high standard, but all these turned out to be the last new half-cab saloons for Tramways. Shown here is No. C2747 standing in Anchor Road; a popular location for off-service buses.

Michael Mogridge

Plate 63:   In the spring of 1950, BBW produced a batch of ten coach bodies mounted on 1937 J chassis. Nine replaced Duple coachwork on JO6As and JO5Gs, Nos. 2201—9 *(see Plate 8)*, while one replaced a Bristol saloon body on JO5G No. 2060 (EHT 98). No. 2202 (DHY 654), a JO6A, is seen here behind Bath Spa Station, and offers a comparison with the 1948 L6B alongside *(see also Plate 45)*. The Bristol body, it will be noticed, now incorporated ECW's pattern of cab, bulkhead, rear-end, etc., but featured square-cornered vents; furthermore it used the same metal framing. Bus versions of this body appeared later in 1950. These coaches, like their L6B cousins, were modified to B35R by 1954.

P. R. Forsey

Plates 64a & 64b: Bristol Tramways repainted four buses in experimental liveries in March 1950. L6A No. 2183 (JHT 836) *(top)* and K6B No. C3409 (KHT 515) *(centre)* received an unrelieved all over green, as can be seen. On the other hand, No. C3415 (LAE 319) had cream relief applied to the window surrounds, instead of the two bands, in the same fashion as No. C5000 *(see Plate 53)*. Fourthly, No. 3733 (LAE 310) gained cream window surrounds and, also, the band above the lower deck windows. The two all-green buses shown, received much unfavourable comment, naturally, but the scheme applied to No. 3733 was so well appreciated that the pattern was adopted for all double deckers repainted later in 1950 and during 1951.

Michael J. Tozer

Plate 65: The cheerful new livery of 1950/1 had quite a beneficial effect on the appearance of the buses. A 1938 K5G/ECW No. C3153 (FHT 74) shows how the cream relief on the window surrounds made the rather heavy-looking pre-war Ks somewhat less overbearing. Incidentally, 1950 saw a start being made at withdrawing the unrebodied pre-war Ks, which were the oldest complete double deckers in the fleet.

Michael J. Tozer

Plate 66: The 1950/1 livery particularly suited the post-war ECW body, as can be seen in this view of Leyland PD1 No. C4016 (KHW 627). The bus is set among the wartime 'prefabs' at the Hengrove end of the 3A service; a few years later this route was merged with the 10A to form route 11.

R. F. Mack

Plate 67: Another body to be improved by the 1950/1 livery was the 1949 Bristol product of rather upright and stern features, mounted on forty of the pre-war K5Gs. No. C3109 (EHY 571) had, as its Eastville depot stablemates, the 25 not dissimilar-looking BBW Leyland PD1s *(see Plate 43)*. The bus is seen at Sea Mills.

Michael Mogridge

Plate 68: The year 1950 saw the end of an era, as all remaining B types were withdrawn. One of those affected was No. 555 (AHU 958), a 1934 bus with all-metal B30D bodywork. It is pictured in Bath depot yard; compare this view with *Plate 1*.

Michael J. Tozer

The Territorial Changes of 1950

In the early years of its existence, the British Transport Commission rationalised the operating areas of some of its subsidiaries and in May 1950, Bristol Tramways was involved in some territorial exchanges. On a pre-1950 map, its services in Gloucestershire appeared to have a 'hole' in the middle, comprising Stroud and the surrounding valleys. Services here were provided by two other operators — one was the Western National Omnibus Company which, like BT&CC, had been a Tilling Company. Its rapidly expanding ancestor, the National Omnibus & Transport Company, had chosen Stroud to be its first stepping stone into the West of England, while the Great Western Railway also once ran bus services here. Under the terms of a 1928 Act of Parliament, the GWR and other railway companies acquired 50 per cent of the shares in various bus companies in their regions, in exchange for the railway bus services *(see also the Foreword to this book)*. Insofar as the extensive National Omnibus & Transport Company was concerned, it was decided to form separate companies in each principal railway company's territory, and this resulted, in the south-west, in the formation of Western National and Southern National in 1929, with shareholdings by the Great Western Railway and the Southern Railway respectively.

Red & White Services Ltd., the other operator in Stroud, had been a privately-owned company with headquarters in Chepstow, Monmouthshire. Their services largely covered Monmouthshire and parts of Glamorgan, but they also had this outpost in Stroud. Many services in the Stroud area were jointly operated by Red & White and Western National, Bristol only getting a look in at the time on the 51 service from Gloucester via Stonehouse, the 58 service from Gloucester via Painswick and the 46 service from Cheltenham via Painswick; even then the latter was jointly worked with Western National, who numbered it 220.

Red & White actually had quite an empire, with several bus operators in businesses throughout South Wales and Southern England. One of these was Cheltenham District Traction Company, who provided this glorious spa's town services amidst Bristol Tramways' Country routes. Red &

White had decided to sell out the bus operating businesses to the B.T.C., in the belief that if nationalisation was inevitable, a voluntary sale might result in a better financial deal.

The territorial changes that occurred in May 1950, saw the transfer lock, stock and barrel of both the Red & White and Western National holdings at Stroud, to Bristol Tramways. Similarly, control of Cheltenham District passed to BT&CC. On the other hand, BT&CC lost their services in the Forest of Dean, including Coleford depot, to Red & White on 1st January 1951. The buses involved in this deal were soon returned to Tramways, while Red & White regained their saloons from Stroud.

In terms of other vehicles which changed hands, Western National provided the expected selection of Bristols and these included some very new Ks. There were also some small Dennises (very popular with that Company), Bedford OWBs, Bedford OB coaches and modernised early 1930s Leylands. Red & White's contribution, conversely, was largely based on Albion chassis, with a few Bedford OB coaches and just one Bristol, a rare GO6G. The Cheltenham District fleet tended to reflect Red & White buying policy, consisting of pre and post-war Albions and wartime Guys, with some AEC Regents and, best of all, some very fine Guy Arab IIIs, still in the course of delivery.

Two small operators were acquired by Bristol Tramways in 1950, both being in the Bristol area. Henry Russett of Brislington, Bristol, ran a haulage business, together with a small coach fleet which traded under the name 'Royal Blue' — a well-known fleetname elsewhere in the West! Russett's lorry fleet was nationalised through the Road Haulage Executive, and so passed to British Road Services. At the same time, the fleet of Bedford coaches and one rarity — a Foden — were passed to Bristol Tramways. Finally, the last independent stage carriage operator to run into Bristol fell to Tramways, this being Ball of Dundry ('Dundry Pioneer'). No vehicles were acquired, but a new Bedford Mulliner saloon was on order and was delivered direct to Tramways.

Plate 69: The oldest double decker acquired with Western National's Stroud operations was this 1931 Leyland TD1 (FJ 7835) bought new by Exeter Corporation. Western National bought it in 1945 and later fitted a 5LW engine, a Covrad long radiator and this new, but old-fashioned, Beadle body in 1947. For convenience, BT&CC reissued fleet number L3600 for it, not intending to keep it long. Indeed, when photographed in September 1950, still with Western National names, it had only two months to live. However, the 1947 Beadle body then displaced the 1943 Brush body on 1941 K5G No. C3352 (GHU 489), seen in *Plate 29*. This new combination was numbered L4138 and returned to Stroud. After withdrawal in 1955, No. L4138 saw further service with Southern Vectis. Even after that, it passed through at least three independents in East Anglia before being scrapped in 1959.

Peter Davey

Plate 70: Seven little Dennises of 1934—37 were numbered 657—663 after Bristol's own Maces *(see Plate 9)*. However, all except No. 657 were normal control Aces. No. 659 (ATT 191), with Brush B20F bodywork, clearly shows the long snout of these buses, which earned them the nickname 'Flying Pig'.

Bristol Vintage Bus Group Collection

Plate 71: Thirteen Bristol saloons were also taken over (Nos. 2485—97); seven were 1933 Hs — a model built in large numbers for National — now with 5LWs and 1940—3 Bristol bodies, the latter to National's own distinctive design. The other six were 1936 JO5Gs, with 1948/9 Beadle B36R bodies. Surprisingly, the Hs were withdrawn in 1951 while the Js fared better, except for one whose body moved to No. 2367 *(see Plate 58)* in 1952, returning to Stroud with its new chassis. The rest were fitted with PV2 radiators, as exemplified by No. 2495 (ADV 121) seen in 1954, and lasted until 1958. In the background of this view is a Western National KS5G, which has run in on route 223 from Trowbridge, Wilts. thus still representing that operator in Stroud. Trowbridge itself was to fall to Bristol in 1970.

Peter Davey

Plate 72: In addition to No. L3600 (see Plate 69), the other eleven ex-Western National double deckers were all Bristol Ks, which became Nos. L4127—37. Three were pre-war, two of which carried ECW bodies of Western National's own styling. Many firms 'designed' their pre-war ECW single deck bodies (see Plates 7 and 41), but few Tilling companies did not take a version of ECW's standard double decker; compare this with Plate 65. No. L4129 (DOD 504) is seen in Stroud, after receiving Tramways' livery and destination box. By this time, the routes had been renumbered from the 200s to the 400s — service 421 could be regarded as the 'trunk' service.

Peter Davey

Plate 73: Fortunate acquisitions from Western National were eight post-war K5Gs and K6Bs, most of which were only a matter of months old and therefore featured 'thin-wall' bodies and London seats. One such bus, No. L4136, had been diverted from the Caledonian Omnibus Company to Western National, on the occasion of the former being taken over by Western SMT. Its registration, LTA 723, was the first of a block of 277 LTA marks issued to National! The bus is seen just after take-over, when the addition of the Tramways fleet numbers was the only appearance change from its Western National days.

Peter Hulin

Plate 74: About ten years after acquiring them, Bristol decided to transfer the front registration plates of the post-war Ks from Western National's favourite position, at the foot of the radiator, to the conventional site on the front dash. In this 1960 view, No. L4132 (KUO 945) has been modified, while No. L4133 (KUO 959) and L4136 (LTA 723) remain to be altered. Note the neat but obviously home-made destination boxes.

Allan Macfarlane

Plate 86: A final act, before Red & White bowed out of CDTC, was the transfer of one of their lowbridge buses to Cheltenham for the Hatherley route. Numbered 79 (GWO 884), it was a 1949 Albion Venturer bodied, appropriately enough in view of future events, by ECW! In this 1960 view, taken in the lane leading to the St. Marks depot, No. 79 reflects the telegraph wires alongside the former Midland Railway line. The bus lasted until as late as 1965.

Allan Macfarlane

Plate 87: The 1934—6 AEC Regents, taken over with the CDTC stock, were soon taken out of service, but three of them, No. 5 (DG 9822), No. 7 (BAD 27) and No. 8 (BAD 28) appeared in August 1950 in a very different form. Now rebuilt to open top, repainted cream with two green bands and renumbered 3610—2, they inaugurated an open top seafront service at Weston-super-Mare. They worked route 152 between the Old Pier, Grand Pier and Sanitorium. The first is seen here, in September 1950, at the Old Pier.

Fred Lloyd

Plate 88: The coach operating business of Henry Russett of Brislington, Bristol, known as Royal Blue, was passed to Bristol Tramways in 1950 when Russett's haulage fleet was nationalised. The deal involved nine Bedford/Duples, as well as one Plaxton-bodied Foden PVSC5! New in 1948, LAE 906 was powered by a Gardner 5LW engine and was given fleet number 2200, a number that, for some reason, had never been used before. Tramways operated their sole Foden until 1955.

Michael Mogridge

Plate 89: The former Russett Bedfords, Nos. 281—289, varied in vintage from 1935 to 1949. The newest was MHT 597, a Vista-bodied OB. It is seen here, in Queen Square, with its number 289 carried on Russett's Royal Blue livery. All Russett Bedfords were sold by 1954.

R. F. Mack

Plate 90: No vehicles were exchanged when the one route business of Dundry Pioneer was acquired from S. A. & W. F. Ball. This service was the last independently-worked route running into Central Bristol, linking the City with the village of Dundry, high on a hill to the south, via Winterstoke Road, Bishopsworth and a steep lane at the Dundry end. On order, however, was a new Bedford OB, this being bodied by Mulliner to B31F layout. The bus was accordingly delivered to Tramways, and numbered 219 (MHU 915). It initially maintained the Dundry service (now blended with Bristol's route 80), sometimes relieved by one of BT&CC's Duple OBs *(see Plate 59)*, but is seen here at Weston-super-Mare. It was withdrawn in 1956, being amongst the first OB saloons to go.

Geoff. Gould, Courtesy Bristol Vintage Bus Group

Plate 91: Under new regulations introduced in 1950, the overall length of double deckers was increased from 26ft. to 27ft., while single deckers increased from 27ft. 6in. to 30ft. An overall width of 8ft. was now permitted, 7ft. 6in. previously being allowed. Built to the new dimensions were Bristol's LL and LWL single deck chassis, and the KS and KSW double deck chassis, W indicating wide, of course. ECW restyled their double deck bodywork to produce a handsome four bay design with large windows, resulting in one of the most attractive buses of the period. The seating capacity was raised to sixty. The City fleet received 22 KS6Bs, of 7ft. 6in. width, during 1950/1, numbered C3456—77 (NAE 11—32), of which No. C3477 is seen here at Knowle West. Seven more were intended for Country services, although only No. 3784 was allocated there before it was decided to place them in the Gloucester fleet, as Nos. 1520—6 (NAE 33—9) instead.

Michael Tozer

Plate 92: While deliveries of the KSs were progressing, the first eight KSWs were activated on trunk Country routes. Tramways decided to draw attention to their 8ft. width in two ways; one by fitting a white steering wheel, and the other by starting a completely new numbering series — at 8000! Seen here, when new, is the third KSW to be built, No. 8002 (NAE 62), working the Bristol to Bath 33 service. The eight KSWs were followed by eighteen 'hybrid' buses — KS6Bs with 8ft. wide bodies, Nos. 8008—25 (NAE 40—57).

Michael Mogridge

Plate 93: A new design of coach body was introduced by ECW in 1950, having the flowing lines favoured by Duple and many others for some years. Known as 'Queen Mary' coaches in many areas, they appeared during the change-over from L to LL/LWL chassis. BT&CC's last three Ls, Nos. 2465—7 (NAE 1—3), had 31 seat bodies and exposed radiators, and were followed by seven LL6B 35 seaters which were bodied to the 8ft. width. This is clearly detectable here by the overhanging wheel arches. A new numbering system for 8ft. single deckers was started at 2800. In Queen Square the first LL, No. 2801 (NAE 4), is accompanied by the first of the three L6Bs, No. 2465 (NAE 1).

R. F. Mack

Plate 94: A major advance in single deck design was the placing of the engine on its side, between the axles, so allowing a front door to be placed under full supervision of the driver. The new Bristol model was called Light Saloon or LS. The first prototype appeared in 1950, with a horizontal Bristol XWA engine, 7ft. 6in. axles and a 42 seat dual-doorway body. The bus was distinctively painted green below the waist and cream above, and featured the Tilling Group's new three piece destination box at the front, with a side by side layout at the back. Numbered 2800, and having the registration number NHU 2 (NHU 1 was a Rolls-Royce!) it was a regular performer on route 85 to Portishead, where the steep Rownham Hill on the south side of the Avon Gorge was unsuitable for double deckers. The bus is seen after taking up duty in February 1951.

Michael J. Tozer

Plate 95: A series of changes overcame No. 2800 between 1951 and 1956. Amongst other things, the Bristol engine was replaced by a Gardner 5HLW, full-width axles were installed, the rear doorway was removed (making it B44F), it was repainted in standard green with a cream band and, finally, BT&CC's current single piece destination boxes were fitted. In this form, No. 2800 spent its remaining years up to 1967 at Wells or Weston-super-Mare, where it is seen here. Note the curve to the base of the windscreen, as if rising over a radiator — old habits die hard!

Allan Macfarlane

Plate 96 (above): In June 1951, the post-war programme of fitting new bodies to old chassis finally drew to a close. Up to this time 103 Gs, one H, 134 Js, forty Ks and eight Ls had been given new coachwork, as seen in *Plates 38, 44, 54—57 and 63.* The last new bodies, built by BBW during 1951, copied ECW products even down to the type of sliding ventilators, although a keen eye could easily detect the differences. The last new body was mounted on a 1936 chassis, numbered JO6A.1, belonging to No. 2003 (CAE 955). The freshly-completed bus is seen leaving the public weighbridge in the Haymarket, subsequently the site of Lewis' store.

Michael Mogridge

Plate 97: In 1951, the five ex-Exeter Corporation GO5Gs, Nos. 3663—7, *(see Plate 40)*, now with 1948 ECW H56R bodies, were transferred to Gloucester and renumbered 1527—31. The first is seen here in King's Square.

Peter Davey

Plate 98: Yet more double deckers were transferred to Gloucester later in 1951. These were three 1939 K5Gs, from the Bath Electric Tramways fleet, where they had been Nos. 3802/7/12 (GL 6603/8/13). The latter bus, now No. 1534, is also seen at King's Square. They were withdrawn in July 1952, being replaced by three post-war K5Gs from Country services.

Peter Davey

Plate 100: Seven further buses with pre-war Bristol bodies, set to work in Weston during 1951/2, had some people baffled about their identity. They looked like pre-war Ks now fitted with PV2 radiators, but the sharp rasping to their exhausts and HHU/HHW registrations were heavy clues to their true origins — they were, in fact, wartime Guy Arabs, such as that seen in *Plate 23!* No. 3630 (HHU 352), seen in this view, carries the body from No. C3220 (FHT 264). Another of these bodies was mounted on Cheltenham District Arab No. 54 (FAD 255) but this, like No. 3638 (HHW 13), retained its Guy radiator.
Peter Davey

Plate 101: The first Bristols to be placed in the Cheltenham District fleet, two KSW6Bs, entered service during late 1951/early 1952. Purely by chance, these first 8ft. buses had fleet numbers beginning with an 8, as their numbers 80 and 81 were simply the next in the sequence. No. 80 (NHY 938) was the more interesting bus, as it had lowbridge bodywork for route 12, on which it joined the lowbridge ECW-bodied Albion No. 79 *(see Plate 86).*

R. F. Mack

Plate 102: KSWs for the City, Country and Bath Services fleets arrived in large numbers totalling, by mid-1953, well over 100 buses, with very many more to follow. Unlike previous types, the KSWs for these divisions were numbered together in the 8000 series. Ten of the 1952 buses were novel in being lowbridge, and were to be the only low-bridge KSWs other than CDTC's No. 80. Numbered L8086—L8095, six ultimately ran for Bath Services including No. L8090 (OHY 939), seen here on the Bath and Salisbury route. These were some of the first buses with enclosed platforms and saloon heaters, while five of the ten intro-duced the Gardner 6LW-engined KSW6G variant to the fleet.

Michael Mogridge

Plate 103: Although the Motor Constructional Works introduced the LS model as successor to the L class in 1952, Tramways' operating fleet ordered ten more LWL6B 'Queen Mary' coaches for that season. Numbered 2818—27 (OHY 990—999), their chassis constituted the entire 95th Sanction — only Wilts & Dorset had later LWLs. Note the route information board above the side windows of No. 2820.

R. H. G. Simpson

Plate 104: The LS eventually arrived in the Tramways fleet in 1953, and included the first saloons since the 1950 Ls and prototype LSX. The first example, No. 2828 (PHW 918), caused a stir when it arrived in full London Transport Green Line livery; it was destined for evaluation trials with London Transport, from April 1953, for one year. Before departing for the Metropolis, No. 2828 did service trials at home, and is pictured here at the Old Bridge stance, while on loan to Bath Tramways.

P. R. Forsey

Plate 105: It wasn't until the end of 1953 that LS saloons started entering service in quantity and, in contrast to the preceding two, they carried Bristol's standard single piece destination box. No. 2847 (PHW 937) carries a less than fully utilised destination display, as it journeys across the northern edge of Salisbury Plain on Bath Services' route 41. After withdrawal in 1968, this bus became Eastern Counties' No. LM582.

Bristol Vintage Bus Group Collection

Plate 106: The first LS coaches entered service in 1953 (2858–67: PHW 948–57). They were destined to be the only Bristol-engined LS6Bs in the fleet (they had been the first to be built, too) and came in a dramatic livery of cream and black. A similar livery adorned the LS coaches of Crosville and Tillings. There was no question about their suitability for express work, as demonstrated by No. 2859 pictured at Hants & Dorset's Fareham bus station whilst en route to Southsea. But for excursions and tours, to such places as Cheddar Gorge, it was regrettable that Bristol's coaches never featured cant panel windows.

Surfleet

Plate 107: Another interesting arrival in 1953 was the first pre-production Lodekka, No. L8133 (PHW 958). It was vastly different from prototype No. LC5000 *(see Plate 53),* and set the standards for production Lodekkas. It was the first Bristol with what was called a 'New Look' front, with a wide cowl and bonnet, although the pattern of the grille and the curvature of the bonnet top were modified on production models *(see Plate 113).* This open platform 58 seater initially ran on Bristol Country services (service 27 was a lowbridge route), as seen here in Queen Square, but was transferred to Bath Services in 1956. Incidentally, it retained this grille until just one month before withdrawal!

Michael J. Tozer

Plate 108: Seldom were buses transferred between City and Country services, particularly since the war. By the early 1950s, however, the City single deck fleet of Nos. C2701—60 had become too large, so in 1952 the Js, Nos. C2701—4/31, became Bath Services' new Nos. 2215—9. In 1953, the six newest Ls of 1950, Nos. C2755—60 (MHW 982—7) were transferred to Country services. They were renumbered 2471—6, and here No. 2475 gets into difficulties in the snow on Failand, the high ground south of Bristol.

Peter Davey

Plate 109: The use of pre-war bodies to replace wartime utility bodies continued, in 1953, with more interesting results *(see Plate 100)*. Three of the lowbridge 1941 Duple bodies from ex-Red & White Albions were mounted on 1945 K6As Nos. L3644/7/51 *(see Plates 32 and 77)*. They were to remain in this condition only until 1955/6. No. L3644 (HHY 588) was pictured, appropriately, at Stroud.

Bristol Vintage Bus Group Collection

Plate 110: Cheltenham District's wartime Guys were also involved in body changes. As mentioned in *Plate 100*, No. 54 received a 1938 Bristol body, while handsome 1940 Weymann bodies from Albion Venturers were fitted to Nos. 51, 57 and 60. That on No. 51 came from No. 33, while No. 57 took the body from No. 3783, the ex-Red & White bus *(see Plate 76)*. The most odd was No. 60 (EWO 751), which was new to Red & White; this not only gained the body from No. 30, shown in *Plate 80*, but also received a Bristol radiator! The outcome is seen here, but it only survived another two years.

Fred Lloyd

Plate 111: A start was made at withdrawing the Gs and Js with post-war bodies in 1954, only three years after the last was rebodied! However, withdrawals were not carried out thoughtlessly, as further use was made of the 1948—50 ECW bodies and 1950/1 single deck Bristol bodies. These were transferred to various Ks and Ls, in a carefully-evolved plan, the first to benefit being some of the 1949 B replacement L5Gs *(see Plate 51).* Seen at Swainswick near Bath, in January 1955, No. 2299 (HW 9493) has become an all-1949 product, having received the ECW body from No. 2039 (CHU 564).

P. R. Forsey

Plate 112: The ECW bodies from the Gs were used, initially, to replace the utility bodies on the 1944—6 Ks (the few K5Gs were modified to K6A or K6B at the same time, the engines for these and some post-war K5Gs being exchanged with all L6As and some of the L6Bs). The lowbridge buses *(Plates 32 and 109)* were given new fleet numbers at the end of their series, on receiving highbridge bodies. These bodies, incidentally, were perceptibly higher at the front than at the back, when mounted on the K chassis, due to their 'square' windscreens. No. 3793 (HHY 595) carries the body from No. 1530 (BFJ 158) on the chassis of No. L3651, shown in *Plate 32.*

Allan Macfarlane

Plate 113: It was 1955 before Tramways took its first production Lodekkas — a year later than many B.T.C. firms, as the KSW was still the preferred choice. The first 22 Lodekkas (LD6Bs THW 731—52) were shared between CDTC (No. 89), Bath Tramways (Nos. L8242—7) and, with enclosed platforms, Bristol Country services (Nos. L8248—62). The latter were particularly associated with Wells and Stroud, and offered a welcome relief to travellers on their lowbridge routes such as service 137, on which No. L8253 is seen at the Prince Street, Bristol, terminus. After withdrawal in 1970, this bus passed to Thames Valley. Curiously, all BT&CC LDs retained the 58 seat capacity of the original design.

Geoff. Gould, Courtesy Bristol Vintage Bus Group

Plate 114: By 1955, the coach fleet had become very modern, comprising 55 units all built since 1950 and all but three being 8ft. wide. The last of the 25 LS coaches were Nos. 2878—82 (THY 952—6), which were LS6Gs, like the previous year's Nos. 2868—77 (SHT 341—50). No. 2878 is seen here, on a Bath city tour, in June 1960.

P. R. Forsey

Plate 115: Two LS saloons became test-rigs for their manufacturers. Chassis No. 89.112, with dual-door body, worked for the Motor Constructional Works (which became the independent Bristol Commercial Vehicles Ltd. in 1955, although still under B. T. C. control), while ECW had No. 97.093 to help in the development of the small SC4LK. Both LSs passed to Tramways' operating fleet in 1955, as Nos. 2883 and 2884 (UHT 493 and UHT 494) respectively. While being fitted out prior to delivery, trial engines were experimentally installed; No. 2883 gained a Commer two-stroke, three cylinder motor (LS. TS. 3) while No. 2884 received an AEC AH470 engine (LS6A) and AEC gearbox, both as used in AEC's Reliance. No. 2884's body featured certain SC ideas, such as sparse ventilation, lightweight seats and side by side destination sites; with its AEC engine, it was a lively bus! No. 2883's Commer unit was soon replaced by a 5HLW, but No. 2884 remained an LS6A until after sale in 1969. During heavy overhaul a few years earlier, No. 2884 received an MW type radiator grille.

Allan Macfarlane

Plate 116: New buses entering service from August 1955 (starting with the UHY batch) carried a shallower destination box, reduced from 18in. to 12in., while remaining 36in. wide. It is shown well in this view of KSW6B No. C8322 (UHY 362), delivery of which took the City's KSW total above 175 units, but with still plenty more to come. The UHY registration series, at 99 marks (UHY 341—439) was the largest block ever issued to BT&CC. Route 18, on which No. C8322 is seen, had its origins in the Company's first bus route.

R. H. G. Simpson

Plate 117: Although the City fleet was predominantly highbridge, lowbridge buses were needed for the 36/236 route, because of West Town Lane Bridge in Knowle. (The same railway, the former Bristol & North Somerset — in which BT&CC's George White had a financial stake — on crossing the road at Pensford, south-east of Bristol, also caused the 27 and 136/137/237 circuit to use lowbridge buses — *see Plates 107 and 113*). In 1955, the City received its first seven Lodekkas, Nos. LC8271—7 (UHY 398—404), to replace the utility Ks LC3374—8 and the odd Country K on these routes. Of the new LDs, Nos. LC8273 and LC8275 featured a new shorter grille, which also appeared on Country buses from No. L8282. Seen outside 'The Tatler' cinema in Carey's Lane, when new, No. LC8277 displays the initial type of blind for the 12in. boxes, with only two intermediate points.

Michael J. Tozer

Plate 118: Having received one Lodekka early in 1955, Cheltenham District resumed delivery of KSWs for the next two batches; Nos. 90 and 91 (UHY 374 and UHY 375) in late 1955, and Nos. 92 and 93 (WHW 821 and WHW 822) in 1956. Whereas the preceding Bristols, Nos. 80—89, had used Bristol engines, a switch was made hereafter to Gardner 6LWs, for all but one of CDTC's buses over the next eleven years. No. 91, with only two intermediate points on its blinds, was photographed at the St. Marks terminus of route 2 when one month old.

Les Lapper

Plate 119: The Gloucester city fleet did not receive its first 8ft. bus until late 1955, when KS No. 8025 (NAE 57) was transferred from Country services. It started a new numbering series at 1800, and was soon followed by four sisters (although No. 1801 was a KSW (NAE 61)). In this view, No. G1802 (NAE 43), formerly No. 8011, is seen in 1960 after receiving the G prefix, and is accompanied by No. G1545 (JHT 121), a rebodied wartime K — *see Plates 35, 112 and 97*, the latter depicting the same body, on No. 1527.

Allan Macfarlane

Plate 120: A series of pre-war Ls was chosen to receive bodies from Js around 1955. First treated were the 1941/2 Country and Gloucester L5Gs (HAE, HHT and DFH registrations) which still carried their original bodies, the Bath and City examples having already been withdrawn. Next, some of the 1938/9 Ls, which had already received new Bristol bodies in 1949 were, during 1956/7, given 1949 ECW or 1950/1 Bristol bodies! One of these was No. G1254 (CFH 604) which, in this view, carries a 1950 Bristol body which was initially a coach (note the extra beading) on No. 2208 (DHY 660) *(see Plate 63).*

Allan Macfarlane

Plate 121: During 1955, by way of assessment, a 1938 ECW-bodied K5G, No. C3135 (FAE 602), received a PV2 radiator, an AEC 7.7 litre engine, the 1950 H59R body from No. C3000 (HY 3630) featured in *Plate 39* and the new fleet number of C3483. (The chassis number was 4543, and the body number 4544!). Seen in its modernised form in Westbury-on-Trym — Mogford's shop is just the same today — No. C3483 only lasted until 1960, but then became driver trainer No. W101 until 1966.
Allan Macfarlane

Plate 122: Production of the K class Bristol drew to a close in 1957, twenty years after it started. As it happened, the first K, No. C3082 (EAE 280), with chassis No. K5G. 42.1, was still in service, albeit now with a 1949 Bristol body. It was therefore brought to meet the final KSW, No. C8431 (YHT 927), with chassis No. KSW6G.118.037, as can be seen. KSWs themselves remained in service until 1976. Another important event of 1957 was the change of the Company's title, to Bristol Omnibus Company Ltd.
Michael J. Tozer

Plate 123: The maximum length of double deckers was extended from 27ft. to 30ft. in 1956, and Bristol Commercial Vehicles Ltd. built six 30ft. Lodekkas, in 1957, for assessment. They had a capacity of seventy, and featured air-brakes. They were shared between several B. T. C. firms, Bristol's one bus being No. L8450 (YHT 962). It originally ran on the Bristol to Weston route 24, but was transferred to Bath Services in 1963.
Geoff. Gould, Courtesy Bristol Vintage Bus Group

Plate 124: In an attempt to counter the drop in revenue, following the decline in passenger traffic that had started everywhere earlier in the 1950s, the Company introduced one-man-operation of single deckers, in 1957, on lightly-trafficked routes. For the purpose, some L5Gs were rebuilt with forward entrances and cut-away bulkheads; the buses treated happened to be receiving replacement bodies around that time. No. 2385 (LHT 903) was new in 1948 as an L6B coach *(see Plate 45)* but gained a 1951 Bristol body which was converted to one-man-operation. It is seen at Weston-super-Mare Station, on town service No. 93, the first route to receive one-man-operated Ls. Interestingly, another conversion involved No. 2082 (FAE 56) of 1938, this being the very first L!

Michael J. Tozer

Plate 125: The MW model appeared in 1958, as successor to the LS *(see Plate 105)*. The bodies of the first batch of MWs, Nos. 2930—50 (920—40 AHY) featured ugly flat backs; cream relief was applied to the window surrounds. After only five had been delivered, a new style of destination box appeared on No. 2935. This was T-shaped, a layout growing in popularity, to minimise the cost of linens. Bristol's was unique, though, in retaining the 36in. width and using a four track number box. An excellent impression of these buses is given by this view of Nos. 2934 and 2938. They stand on the forecourt of the new Marlborough Street Country bus and coach station (originally known as Whitson Street), opened on 21st September 1958 to replace terminal points in Prince Street, The Centre and Old Market. A bus station had been opened in Bath in the March.

Peter Davey

Plate 126: Having introduced T type destination boxes on its new buses, B. O. C. set about rebuilding earlier double deckers with this type in 1959. Initially they concentrated on City buses. Massive route changes had occurred there on 21st September 1958 — this being the biggest single overnight change in the history of bus services! Most routes were linked to become cross-city, causing the loss of such numbers as 132/232 and 138/238. The B. O. C.-made box was unusual in having a small, single track route number blind, although in the event, it was applied only to City KSWs, one Country K (No. 3780), one KS (No. 1525) and one Country KSW (No. 8337). No. C8050 (NHY 972) exemplifies this box in a busy scene at St. James' Barton roundabout, at the top of The Haymarket; the buildings to the right have now given way to the remarkable new complex which spans North Street.

Geoff. Stainthorpe

Plate 127: After all wartime utility bodies had been replaced, early post-war ECW bodies were then scrapped in favour of those from the many remaining Gs. Nos. C3385—96 *(see Plate 37)* were amongst the first treated, having also gained six cylinder engines. The remaining bodies were then mounted on the earliest Ks already powered by six cylinder motors. This patchy selection involved many 1947 buses, such as K6A No. 3836 (KHU 617), seen here in 1964 with a year's service still ahead of it *(see Plate 46).* The body on this bus came from No. 3821 (DKN 38).

R. F. Mack

Plate 128: While rebuilding Ls for one-man-operation *(see Plate 124)*, the Company realised that six Country buses already had a door at the front, these being the B33D L5Gs Nos. 2471—6 *(see Plate 108)*. Rebuilding them to B35F one-man-operation was so successful that twelve City dual-door Ls were rebuilt this way, emerging in 1959 as Country buses Nos. 2479—90. No. 2481 (LHY 983), formerly No. C2743, was one of only four one-man-operated L6Bs (all others had 5LW engines), and stands at Bristol bus station when newly out-shopped.

Allan Macfarlane

Plate 129: In exchange for the City Ls rebuilt to one-man-operation Country buses, twelve similar vintage Country Ls were transferred to the City, in which fleet they were novel in having rear entrances. They were renumbered C2755—66 *(see Plate 108)*. Seen shortly after arrival is No. C2762 (MHW 991), formerly No. 2456. It stands at the Prince Street terminus of route 239, one of few services to retain a central terminal point after the 1958 changes *(see Plate 126)*. Even this was short-lived, as in September 1961 the 239, which was restricted by a very low bridge, was linked to the similarly-restricted service 139 (Old Market to Stapleton) to form route 19. These Ls remained on route 19 until 1965.

Allan Macfarlane

Plate 130 (below): The 1949—51 bodies from Js were remounted on several post-war Ls from 1957 *(see Plates 111 and 124)*. However, the policy was discontinued in 1959, and the last few Js were sold complete with those bodies. No. 2272 (LHT 916), of 1948, was one of the later buses treated, and here carries the 1951 Bristol body from No. 2058 (EHT 544). The cab nearside window is an instant identifier of its J type origins *(see Plate 57)*. It was photographed at Salisbury, while working on an Exeter to Salisbury coach relief!

R. L. Wilson

Plate 131: In 1958, Gloucester Corporation 'mentioned' to the B. O. C. that the local fleet had no buses newer than 1951 vintage, all additions since that year having been transfers. Consequently, B. O. C. ordered three new LDs for them for 1959, this marking the start of a regular intake of three or, later, four new buses each year (this did not exclude the occasional transfer, however). In the meantime, transferred from Bath Services were seven other LDs, six being only a few months old. These simply received a G prefix to their existing fleet numbers, heralding a change in Gloucester's numbering system. No. GL8458 (YHT 945), an open platform LD6G, is seen here in King's Square, five months after arrival.

Allan Macfarlane

Plate 132: In July 1959, the Company placed in service sixteen rather different-looking LDs, (961—976 EHW). These not only carried Cave-Browne-Cave heating equipment, utilising two grilles alongside the destination box, but also featured a reduced number of opening windows, which were of the new 'hopper' type. No. LC8522 (976 EHW) is seen here at Filton, when brand-new, and before it was realised what a fuss these buses would cause!

Michael Bennett

Plate 133 (below): A heatwave hit the country a few days after the EHWs appeared. Due to the unfamiliar new CBC equipment releasing hot air into the buses, combined with the inefficient hopper ventilators, some passengers collapsed from heat exhaustion. An emergency plan saw all the EHWs whisked into the works, to exchange their front windows with those from earlier LDs, carrying push-out vents. Later, the fixed lower deck window from the EHWs was swapped with the slider-equipped glazing from the fourth upper deck bay of earlier LDs. The remaining EHW and FHW Lodekkas entered service thus modified, with the later buses, including No. LC8535 (992 EHW), being completed this way by ECW.

R. L. Wilson

Plate 134: An even more interesting 1959 Lodekka was the first prototype forward entrance bus, an FLF6B. It was a seventy seat 30ft. bus, with a flat lower saloon floor and air suspension. Numbered LC8540 (995 EHW), it carried a full complement of hopper vents and originally had a sliding entrance door. After demonstrating for B. C. V. it received some changes, including a jack-knife door. The emergency door was in the centre of the rear wall, familiar on pre-war single deckers, but note the handle at waist level; later buses had it at the foot of the door, to improve advertising space. Seen work-ing from Fishponds on route 11, its usual haunt *(see Plate 66)* No. LC8540 picks up outside Lewis' store, accompanied by a rebodied wartime K.

Allan Macfarlane

Plate 135: The completion of the 1959 Lodekka order *(see Plates 132 and 133)* materialised in 1960 as FS6Gs Nos. L8547—50 (437—40 FHW). Of the many differences, the longer windows were most noticeable, due to the quarter bay ahead of the platform being eliminated. They were also the first buses to be delivered with flashing 'trafficators'. No. L8550 is pic-tured here, among Wilts & Dorset buses, at Salisbury bus station, while working joint route 709, a blending of Bristol's route 70 (Swindon to Marlborough) and Wilts & Dorset's route 9 (Marlborough to Salisbury).

P. R. Forsey

Plate 136: More new double deckers in 1960 were eleven further FLF6Bs, Nos. LC8551—61 (571—81 HHY), for which the Company insisted on having sliding ventilators! Nos. LC8556—61 featured strip lighting for the first time, taking advantage of its brightness to illuminate advertisement panels on the offside. The buses joined No. LC8540 *(see Plate 134)* on route 11, and No. LC8556 is seen on its first day, 1st September 1960.

Allan Macfarlane

Plate 137: The first coaches to be bought for five years were five MW6Gs 2984—8 (289—93 HHU). They carried deep hopper vents, and could otherwise be distinguished from the LSs by the front grille *(see Plate 114)*. Still no cant panel windows were specified.

Geoff. Stainthorpe

Plate 138 (below): The styling of the original MW saloon, such as that found on Bristol's AHYs *(see Plate 125)*, was not well received, so ECW introduced the finer features of the LS on subsequent MWs. The kinked windscreen and grille were easy identifiers, though. The EHY and JHU batches (excepting 981—3 EHY) carried hopper vents, as shown by No. 2504 (526 JHU) at Malmesbury, on the service to Stroud and Gloucester.

R. F. Mack

Plate 139: Having dabbled with FLFs, Bristol returned to shorter buses, although still keeping to forward entrances. These FSFs were primarily used on urban routes. While delivery was in progress, B. O. C. adopted new numbering schemes for forward entrance Lodekkas; 6000s for sixty seat FSFs and 7000s for seventy seat FLFs, with new MWs Nos. 6000—3 becoming Nos. 2500—3, in January 1961, to make way for new buses. Subsequent new Lodekkas were numbered in the new series, but without the L prefix. No. 6020 (719 JHY) was one of three FSF6Gs new to Weston in 1961.

P. J. Relf

Plate 140: In 1960 there was a race to see who would reach number 100 first — Cheltenham District or the Works fleet! In the event, No. W100 was commissioned just before CDTC placed No. L100 in service in October. The bus was the second of a pair of FSF6Gs (705 JHY and 706 JHY). It was not initially proposed to include CDTC buses in the 1961 renumbering, but in March 1961, they became Nos. 6018/9, and all future CDTC buses were numbered in the B. O. C. series.

Fred Lloyd

Plate 141: The last twelve LSs, Nos. 2918—29, together with MWs Nos. 2951—6, had been delivered with 41 coach seats, although otherwise they were identical to the buses. In 1960, it was decided to distinguish the coach-seated vehicles by repainting the roofs cream. LS5G No. 2920 (YHY 78) and MW5G No. 2952 (972 DAE), both owned by Bath Tramways, stand behind Bath bus station when Railway Street was one-way west-bound. In 1961, these dual-purpose vehicles were renumbered into their own series as Nos. 2000—2017.

Allan Macfarlane

Plate 142: In the winter of 1960/1 the Company's coaches started emerging in a new colour scheme of cream with dark red relief (instead of green). Furthermore, they displayed a new fleet-name either side of the Greyhound and hoop motif, reading 'Bristol Greyhound' in attractive script. Shortly afterwards, the sixty coaches were renumbered into their own series as Nos. 2050—2109. In the spring, five new MW6Gs arrived in the new colours and were numbered 2110—4 (403—7 LHT). Here, No. 2113 is seen at the refreshment stop on the green near Maidenhead bus station (sadly, now built on), accompanied by a new Thames Valley FLF.

Geoff. Stainthorpe

Plate 143: In 1961, the City received its first new single deckers since 1950. The five MW5Gs were numbered C2516—20 (351—5 MHU). Three displaced Ls from the Temple Meads Station to Zoo service 17, while the others joined rear entrance Ls on route 19 *(see Plate 129)*. Accordingly, the last dual-door Ls in the City fleet were withdrawn after only eleven years' service, while seven others, surplus to the City's requirements, had become Nos. 2491—5 and Nos. G2496/7 in 1960. The MWs, like post-1960 City Lodekkas, carried only the route numbers at the rear. In this view, No. C2517 is seen outside the Zoo on its first day. From late 1961, the Bristol coat of arms was replaced by a gold block Bristol name.

Allan Macfarlane

Plate 144: At the end of summer 1961, Weston's faithful open top pre-war K5Gs (see Plate 99) were retired. In their place came four new convertible open top FS6Gs, Nos. 8576—9 (866—9 NHT). With their roofs in place, out of season, these all-cream buses worked ordinary services, but maintained route 152 during the summer with open top decks. Here No. 8576 demonstrates the Weston Borough arms, carried on the side panels from 1965. The route subsequently became service 103, and was extended to Uphill.

Allan Macfarlane

Plate 145: After fitting many City KSWs with T type destination boxes, as shown in *Plate 126*, an improved type with four number tracks was introduced in 1960. It was soon applied to the newer double deckers and to MW single deckers Nos. 2930—4 (see Plate 125), (the latter being the only single deckers to be converted). The four track box replaced the single track version by 1964. A few Ks also received this box, and on low-bridge buses, such as No. L4118 (LHU 511), it was mounted very high, interrupting the upper cream band. The photograph was taken at Stroud bus station, which was opened in 1960. The low registration plate of this bus indicates a pre-68th Sanction chassis, uncommon with metal-framed bodies (see Plate 49).

Allan Macfarlane

Plate 146: B. C. V. introduced an attractive new radiator grille for the Lodekka in 1962, Bristol's first batch being Nos. 7061—5 (506—10 OHU). The grille underwent some subtle styling changes over the years, but the original design is shown here on No. 7064. The bus, an FLF6B, is pulling off the stand in Bristol bus station which, at the time, still contained two platforms, with a high wall to encourage the subway to be used. In the late 1960s, the second platform was removed, and buses now load more or less head-on.

Mike Walker

Plate 147: Three examples of a new and uncommon type of single decker entered service in 1962. They were SUS4As, with four cylinder Albion engines and seating for only thirty. Numbered 300—302 (861—3 RAE), they were allocated to Stroud, where they replaced the last Bedford OBs, Nos. 212/3/5 *(see Plate 59).* The last Leyland PD1s were also withdrawn in 1962, incidentally, leaving CDTC with the only non-Bristols. The SUS and SUL models had only been supplied to Western/ Southern National up to this point and, indeed, Bristol was the only other customer for the SUS — another six arriving in 1963/4.

Allan Macfarlane

Plate 148: The dissatisfaction felt by the Company for the hopper ventilator has been shown in *Plates 132, 133 and 136.* Bath decided to go further in 1962, exchanging alternate hopper vents in the EHY and JHU-registered MWs for sliders from other examples. No. 2977 (989 EHY), formerly rigged out solely with hoppers, shows the mixed set that became a distinctive Bath feature.

Allan Macfarlane

Plate 149: One of those odd, unplanned occurrences that happen during overhaul or repair, led to Bath Services' 1956 LD6B No. L8381 (WHY 936) emerging, in 1962, with a long grille from either a THW or a UHY version. The grille was quite out of keeping with the pattern of cab offside window design, etc. *(see Plate 117),* although the bus had always featured a three piece cowl, being to the 116th Sanction.

Allan Macfarlane

Plate 150: Three very unusual double deckers for this part of the country were bought second-hand in 1963. They were Leyland Atlanteans, with lowbridge 73 seat Weymann bodies, that had originated during 1959—1962 with the famous Silver Star Motor Services of Porton Down in Wiltshire. This firm ceased operations in June 1963, and passed its fleet to Wilts & Dorset. The latter required few of the vehicles, so B. O. C. was happy to accept the Atlanteans. Numbered 7997—9 (TMW 853, VAM 944 and 1013 MW), they were put to work on the Bristol to Weston route 24, alongside the LDL *(see Plate 123).* A year later they were transferred to the Bristol to Portishead 85 route, but were unsuccessful, being withdrawn in September 1964 and sold. In this view, No. 7997 is seen leaving Weston bus station.

Geoff. Stainthorpe

Plate 151: The Atlanteans were not the only odd machines to come from Silver Star, as the Company also picked up their 13 seat Trojan! 367 BAA was numbered 2049, and inaugurated a special tourist service in Bath, running between the Roman Pump Room and the Assembly Rooms. It was later painted blue and was renumbered 400 in 1968, to make way for new dual-purpose vehicles. It remained in stock until 1970, when it was replaced by Transit No. 401 *(see Plate 186).*
Allan Macfarlane

Plate 152: In 1963 it was decided to relegate some of the 1957 dual-purpose LS5Gs. To achieve this, some new MW saloons had their 45 bus seats exchanged for the 41 coach seats in the LSs. The MWs entered service, after receiving cream roofs, as Nos. 2018—24, while the LSs, now B45F in bus livery, reverted to their 29XX numbers. No. 2022 (926 RAE) shows how much the back seat obscured rearward visions. When, in turn, relegated to buses in 1968, they started a new series at No. 2400.

Allan Macfarlane

Plate 153: A popular feature around 1963—9 was the fitting of discs to the rear, and sometimes front, wheels of buses. The original trims were of unpainted metal finish, which naturally earned them the nickname of 'dustbin lids'. No. C7130 (823 SHW), pictured at Filton, was one of three FLFs supplied with Leyland 0.600 engines, for assessment (FLF6Ls). Each was allocated initially to a particular route, and compared with an FLF6B and an FLF6G. The findings were reported back to B. C. V. Country Services' No. 7129 worked on route 33 from Bath, while No. C7130/1 ran on the 6 and the 6A/6B respectively. They remained in service for their full 14—15 year term.

Allan Macfarlane

Plate 154: Twenty impressive new coaches took to the road in 1963/4. They were of the new RELH6G model, 36ft. long, 8ft. 2½in. wide and with Gardner 6HLX engines at the rear. They had 45 seats, and with full air suspension gave an excellent ride. There were two batches; Nos. 2115—24 (861—70 UAE), with Nos. 2115—20 having the very first production RE chassis, and Nos. 2125—34 (971—80 WAE). They introduced another new livery of cream and red, which was subsequently applied to the other coaches. No. 2124 pauses at the popular Marlborough refreshment stop en route for London 'via Reading and M4', what there was of it in 1970! They were withdrawn in 1974, principally because of their manual gearboxes, but Western National snapped up all twenty and continued to work all but one on the London services, as often as not!

Allan Macfarlane

Bristol ⬯ *Greyhound*

Plate 155: RELH coaches were being bought by many nationalised fleets at the time, but United Welsh had no old coaches to be replaced by their two RELHs. Instead, they offered their newest MW6Gs for sale . . . and Bristol bought them! Numbered 2135/6 (279/80 ECY), they not only introduced the latest MW coach body to the fleet, but were also the first to have cant panel windows! In this view, No. 2136 prepares to leave Cheltenham coach station, for Paignton, on an express duty.

Allan Macfarlane

Plate 156: Eastern National were the people to thank for some unique Bristol coaches! The former ordered fourteen dual-purpose MW5Gs for 1965, but later offered seven to other firms. Bristol accepted the seven which were completed with 6HLW motors, ECW adapting the bodies so they became 39 seat, cream and red Greyhound coaches! They became Nos. 2137—43 (BHU 91—7C) and the last is seen here, without its Greyhound motif, entering Bristol bus station bound for Cheltenham.

Allan Macfarlane

Plate 157: The Greyhound MWs Nos. 2137—43 were relegated to bus duties in 1971, being renumbered 2427—33. They received bus livery, but retained the 39 coach seats and single line destination boxes. No. 2429 (BHU 93C), formerly No. 2139, is seen in Bristol in NBC leaf green livery, in which they still stood out due to the polished brightwork and stepped beading, reminiscent of the 1948 L coaches *(see Plate 45).* They were withdrawn during 1978/9.

Allan Macfarlane

Plate 158: Of the seven dual-purpose MW5Gs left to go to Eastern National *(see Plate 156),* four turned up, unlicensed, at Lawrence Hill depot in January 1965 (Nos. 1435—8 : JHK 459—62C). They emerged a week later with Bristol names, fleet numbers 2025—8 and registrations BHW 93—6C! They were somewhat smarter than Nos. 2000—24 *(see Plates 141 and 152)* and their T type destination boxes were to the 'Tilling Standard' pattern, with 40in. wide nameboxes and three track route numbers. They were demoted to bus work as Nos. 2405—8 in 1969, later being reseated to B43F and repainted in bus livery. As such, they looked similar to Nos. 2427—33 in *Plate 157.* No. 2026 is seen here at the new Gloucester bus station, which was opened in 1962 to replace one adjacent to King's Square.

Phil Davies

Plate 159: Despite receiving so many diverted or second-hand MW coaches, the Company ordered another seven for 1966. These were Nos. 2144—50 (FHW 150—6D), 31ft. long 39 seaters, with forced-air ventilation and fixed side windows. They also had the improved deeper windscreens *(see Plate 155).* No. 2150 is seen, with No. 2149, behind Bath bus station. They were withdrawn, after a surprisingly short life, during 1973/4.

Allan Macfarlane

Plate 160: Possibly impressed by the ex-Eastern National dual-purpose MWs, B. O. C. ordered no fewer than twelve for 1966, but for the first time with 6HLW engines and, a unique feature, forced-air ventilation; note the squarer dome. They came into their own when the Severn Bridge was opened in September 1966, and a joint service between Bristol and Cardiff was introduced with Red & White. No. 2038 (HAE 270D) is seen here in Cardiff bus station, shortly after the commencement of the route. It carries the gold 'scroll' fleetname introduced in 1965.

Allan Macfarlane Collection

Plate 161: When Cheltenham District took delivery of Nos. 7276 and 7277 (HHW 459D and HHW 460D) in October 1966, it could hardly have been predicted that this all double deck fleet would receive nothing but single deckers for the next nine years! No. 7276 is seen here, in 1968, on what had been route 3. In May 1966, incidentally, CDTC's Bristols Nos. 80—98 were renumbered into the B. O. C. series, reusing numbers 8551—69, with an L prefix as appropriate. Renumbering affected Gloucester at the same time, when Nos. G1800—4 *(see Plate 119)* became G8025/01/11/12/21 — back to their original places.

Allan Macfarlane

Plate 162: 10/66 and all that . . . 1st October 1966, to be more specific, was a sad day, as it witnessed the closure of various chapters. For one thing, it saw the demise of the original Cheltenham District fleet numbering system and with it, the last vehicles ordered under Red & White control. In turn, these were the last non-Bristols in the B.O.C. fleet, except for the Trojan at Bath. Guy Arab III/Duples Nos. 77 and 78 (JDG 789 and JDG 790) were the two replaced by Nos. 7276 and 7277 *(see Plate 161)*, and No. 78, seen here, was the only example to receive a T type destination box and fleet number plates.

Allan Macfarlane

Plate 163: Also on 1st October 1966, the last two L types were withdrawn. One was No. 2291 (LHY 965), a former Bath Services bus with B35R body, while the other was No. 2495 (LHY 976), remarkably a B33D-bodied bus that was previously No. C2736. Both were L5Gs, and with their demise, the Gardner 5LW engine no longer figured in the passenger fleet — after 32 years! The 5HLW was still widely used, of course. No. 2291, one of few Ls to receive the scroll fleetname, stands at Marlbrough Street.

Mike Walker

Plate 164: The end of the road was reached, also on 1st October 1966, for the K type (and 3XXX series numbers), . . . except for one bus. A sole survivor lasted for one more month and, ironically, it was a lowbridge bus! Fittingly, it was one of Stroud's ex-Western National K6Bs, No. L4134 (KUO 963). In this view of Stroud bus station, taken a few years earlier, can be seen, from the left, No. L4136 (LTA 723), No. L4121 (LHU 517), No. L4131 (KUO 932), No. L4125 (LHU 515) and No. L8282 (UHY 411), showing duplication in both directions of the 'trunk' 421 (note the different destination displays).

R. F. Mack

Plate 165: During 1966, while conversions to T type destination boxes were under way, a strange and hardly cheap temporary change was made to Gloucester's city buses and Cheltenham's country vehicles; their single piece screens were overpanelled, to leave just a single line. This is shown here by No. L8286 (UHY 415), a 1955 H58RD-bodied LD6G, which can just be seen working route 542 from Cheltenham to Bishop's Cleeve. Ironically, this bus retained this box until it was withdrawn in 1971!

Graham Jones

Plate 166: The 1966/7 FLFs featured more glassfibre in their bodywork, while the upper cream band was discontinued. Buses for Gloucester, Cheltenham and the City now sported a three track route number box, while the rear T box of Gloucester, Cheltenham, Country and Bath buses was inverted. The 1967 FLFs differed further by not having CBC heaters, the first since 1959. Whereas the 1966 buses had fixed rubber-mounted windscreens, B.O.C. requested opening screens again for 1967. No. C7296 (JHW 64E) displays the unmistakable face of the 1967 FLF (compare the grille with that in *Plate 146*); these were the last Lodekkas built for the Company.

Graham Jones

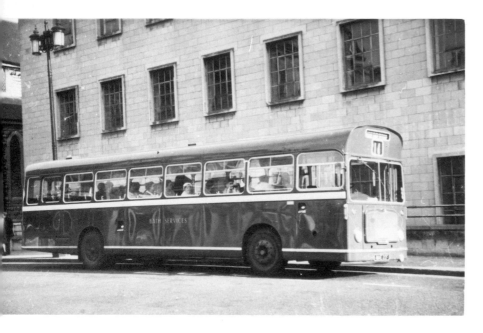

Plate 167: The 36ft. 53 seat RELL saloon was introduced in 1967, intended for one-man-operation and to replace double deckers. Within eighteen months over 100 were in service, running in all fleets except the City, which was awaiting the VR to enter production. The RELLs were numbered 1000 upwards. No. 1019 (MAE 22F) is a Bath Tramways bus, working Bath city route 214. The Leyland O.680 motor was the standard choice of engine for the Company's REs from this point.

Allan Macfarlane

Plate 168: The 1967/8 dual-purpose vehicles were of even higher standards than the 1966 examples *(see Plate 160)*, by using the RELH6L coach as a basis. They were 47 seaters, with Leyland O.680 engines and semi-automatic transmission. Compared with a true coach, they had less brightwork, jack-knife doors and bus destination boxes — Bristols were unique in having T boxes, as No. 2050 (NHW 304F) of 1968 shows. Six of the 1968 order were finished as 45 seat Greyhound coaches Nos. 2151—6 (NHW 308—13F), with a view to future relegation.

Phil Davies

Plate 169: Western National wished to order some FSFs in 1967, but B. C. V. had dropped the FSF in 1963. Bristol Omnibus came to the rescue, however, and sold Western and Southern National twenty of their 38. These FSF6Gs were all the Bath, Country and Cheltenham examples, as well as the first Gloucester bus, and all were repainted and lettered for Western and Southern National at Lawrence Hill. Seen here are 707 JHY, formerly Bath Tramways' No. L6008 and destined to become Southern National No. 1012, and 802 MHW, formerly Cheltenham District's No. 6037 and due to become Western National No. 1011.

Dave Withers

Plate 170: Some of the FSFs sold to Western and Southern National were replaced by new RELLs, but to replace others, some recently withdrawn City KSWs were reinstated, now running for Country or Bath Services. A Bath Services example is No. 8074 (NHY 996, formerly No. C8074), a 1952 KSW6B that gave a year's further service to Bath. *Allan Macfarlane*

Plate 171 (above): A new circular service in Central Bristol was introduced in 1966, worked by Country LSs and MWs with special 'City Centre Circle' headboards. In 1967, four of the newest MW5Gs, Nos. 2628/31/5/6, were allocated to the service, and a special livery was devised. Initially the buses received cream roofs, dual-purpose style, but later the lower panels were also painted cream, producing the scheme shown here by No. 2631 (EAE 470C). It is seen on the Centre, passing the soon to be demolished Sun Life Assurance offices. The C. C. C. was eventually absorbed by other routes.

Allan Macfarlane

Plate 172: It was rather surprising when the City Centre Circle livery was applied to SUS4A No. 305 (845 THY) in 1968! The bus was principally used on the Dundry route, on which Dundry Pioneer once worked (see Plate 90), now service 373. Here No. 305 is seen, in Queen Square, with the usual 'lazy' destination display.

Dave Withers

Plate 173: Another of those unexpected occurrences (see Plate 149) was the appearance, in 1968, of 1956 LD6G No. L8294 (UHY 423) carrying the distinctive grille from pre-production LD No. L8133. It will be recalled that the grille had been removed one month before the withdrawal of No. L8133, earlier in 1968 (see Plate 107). Sadly, No. L8294 received a single piece glassfibre cowl in 1970, and this grille was lost for ever. The bus was pictured, in July 1968, at Keynsham.

Allan Macfarlane

Plate 174: A new version of the popular RE range first appeared in the fleet in 1969, in the form of the RESL6L 43 seater (luggage pens reduced the seating from the maximum available). The first buses, Nos. 500—514 (THU 346—60G), looked like RELLs with one bay missing. They were some of the first REs with taller windscreens, which necessitated the adoption of the 'Tilling Standard' side by side destination box. On these vehicles, hopper ventilators made their return, although these were deeper and alternated with deep sliders. Note the new position of the fleetname on No. 506, pictured outside Bert Bence's old garage in Hanham *(see Plate 25).* After withdrawal just ten years later, No. 506 was among eight of these buses to pass to National Welsh for further service.
Allan Macfarlane

Plate 175: Although one-man-operation of single deckers was almost universal by 1968, it was then decided to introduce a distinctive livery for them, in which the cream was extended down to the skirt panels. The first to appear in this scheme were City MWs but, by 1969, it was affecting other saloons. This included some of the few remaining 1954 LSs (PHW batch), but it is demonstrated here by 1956 bus No. 2887 (XHW 403), photographed at Weston-super-Mare.
Allan Macfarlane

Plate 176 (below): The bright one-man-operated livery had quite a beneficial effect in a thunderstorm as an aid to visibility! No. G2503 (525 JHU), a 1960 MW5G, shows this well. Single deckers played a relatively small part in the Gloucester fleet since the war. Two 1947 L6As were the only new saloons allocated, until some MW5Gs arrived in 1959. In the meantime Bs, rebodied Js and pre-war Ls were transferred to Gloucester in penny numbers. Even after 1959, more Ls arrived. On the advent of their first RELLs, in 1967, only six saloons were operated, comprising four LSs and two MWs. The MW seen here is one of four received in 1971 to replace the LSs.

Allan Macfarlane

Plate 177: The City fleet had received no new buses since its 1967 FLFs *(see Plate 166)*, but had 28 VRs on order. While they were being built, however, the order was changed to 28 RELLs for one-man-operated working, to which were added many of the forthcoming RELLs intended for Country Services. Furthermore, the bodywork was to be of a front entrance/centre exit 44 seat layout. Eager to implement one-man-operation in 1968, the City 'borrowed' some Country B53F RELLs but, in August 1969, amid a blaze of publicity, the first City dual-door buses took over. They were the first to be delivered in one-man-operation livery, and later the destination boxes were opened to the 11in. depth and fitted with informative blinds. This is shown by No. C1112 (UHU 214H) outside the Zoo.

Allan Macfarlane

Plate 178: So keen was the Company on working dual-door REs on urban services that the unique step was taken, after a trial rebuilding, of sending all single-door RELLs from Cheltenham District and Gloucester City, as well as half of Bath Services' specimens, back to ECW for conversion to B44D. They returned in one-man-operation livery (Cheltenham's were dark red and cream, of course) and No. 1087 (OHW 599F), from the Bath Electric Tramways fleet, is shown here. Note the new style fleetname, which was introduced on Bath's single deckers in 1968. While the rebuilding of the RELLs was going on, Bath Electric Tramways Ltd. and Bath Tramways Motor Co. Ltd. ceased trading on 1st December 1969. All assets were transferred to B. O. C., but the Bath Services fleetname was retained by a proportion of the allocation, including dual-door REs.

Allan Macfarlane

Plate 179: A strange purchase, in December 1969, was that of a 1941 K5G open topper! The bus was new as No. C3315 (GHT 127), with ECW H56R body *(see Plate 15)*. It was then sold, in 1955, to Brighton, Hove & District, who rebuilt it as much-modified 59 seat convertible open topper No. 5992, one of many for their seafront service. Sold in 1965 to Thomas Bros. of Port Talbot, for work at Aberafon, it returned to Bristol in 1969. It was not used in service until 1974, when it was numbered 8583, in the 8ft. series! After one season at Weston-super-Mare it received Tilling green livery, for use only on special events. However, it was back on duty at Weston in cream in 1978, this time for two seasons. It is seen in this condition in Ashton Park, Bristol, on an enthusiasts' tour. It was next passed to the Bristol Omnibus Preservation Society, subsequently receiving a facsimile of the pre-war blue and white livery, which, of course, was quite unsuitable for the bus in this condition.

Allan Macfarlane

Plate 180: After helping out Western and Southern National with their FSF requirements in 1967 *(see Plate 169)*, B. O. C. came to the rescue of West Riding Automobile Services, during 1969/1970, by supplying them with 27 FLFs! West Riding, which had been a privately-owned company, had set its faith in the somewhat unconventional Guy Wulfrunian, earlier in the 1960s. For several reasons, this fleet of Wulfrunians was the Company's undoing and, after volunteering the Company's sale to the Transport Holding Company in 1968, a fleet of replacement buses was sought. The new National Bus Company oversaw the transfer of many elderly LD6Gs from member companies, but Bristol supplied 27 of their City FLF6Gs (the other four were retained, as they had just been fitted with two-way radios). Some of the transferred FLFs were as recent as 1966 vintage! One of the older units, however, was 1962 bus No. C7040 (208 NAE), which was photographed at Sea Mills, on a dull December day, during its last month of service with B. O. C.

Allan Macfarlane

Plate 181: Twenty years after the B. T. C. territorial changes saw Western National's outpost at Stroud, in Gloucestershire, pass to the Bristol Company, the B. T. C.'s successor, the National Bus Company, passed Western National's outpost at Trowbridge, in Wiltshire, to the Bristol Company, on 1st January 1970. Again, a varied selection of buses was involved (totalling 24) and remarkably, as in 1950, buses registered LTA were involved! *(see Plate 73).* The oldest transferred were two 1951/2 lowbridge KSW6Bs, (LTA 843 and LTA 844), which B. O. C. numbered L4155/6 in the 7ft. 6in. series! They were somewhat older than any of B. O. C.'s existing KSWs (their own lowbridge ones had been withdrawn during 1967/8), but remained in service several months, before being converted to driver trainers. They are shown here, with Western National names, but Bristol numbers, on 2nd January 1970.

Allan Macfarlane

Plate 182: Eight single deckers passed from Western National, all being 41 seat LS5Gs — and again somewhat older than any B. O. C. was currently operating, except for the last 1954 PHWs, Nos. G2834/5/7/8. The numbers 2409–2416 were given to these LSs. The oldest, dating from 1952, was No. 2412 (LTA 978), which is seen here with dual identities at the bus station. Note where the Western National name has been removed from the building.

Allan Macfarlane

Plate 183: Strangely, Western National deliberately transferred six of their ex-B. O. C. FSFs *(see Plate 169)* to Trowbridge, so they would pass back to B. O. C. With their numbers 1000—5, they logically reverted to their original numbers of 6022—4/30—2. No. 6023 (722 JHY) is seen at Trowbridge on the day after takeover, and again carries Bristol numbers with Western National names.

Allan Macfarlane

Plate 184: The other eight buses taken over were FLF6Bs, which became Nos. 7314—21. Five dated from 1963 and had no CBC heaters, unlike the two 1965 and one 1966 buses. All the FLFs had the 'Tilling Standard' side by side destination boxes, and ventilator layout of hoppers upstairs with deep, alternating hoppers and sliders downstairs. These features made them stand out, especially after all the Lodekkas were moved to Bath, where No. 7317 (820 KDV) is seen in 1978. Sadly, Trowbridge depot and bus station were closed in 1982.

Allan Macfarlane

Plate 185 (above): In May 1970, at which time B. O. C. was committed to a large intake of RELLs, especially for the City fleet, there was the surprising purchase of the two prototype 80 seat VR double deckers. They were powered by 6LX engines, mounted longitudinally in the offside rear corner, and were 33ft. long. Both had been exhibited by their builders at the Commercial Vehicle Show in 1966, No. VRX001 in Central SMT livery (GGM 431D) and No. VRX002 in B. O. C. livery (HHW 933D). They demonstrated for Bristol Commercial Vehicles, before entering in-service trials with Central SMT and Mansfield District, respectively. Before starting work in Bristol, as Nos. C5000 and C5001, they received the double deck version of the one-man-operation livery, as shown here. They were not entirely successful and were sold as early as 1973, passing to an Essex independent.

Dave Withers

Plate 186: In contrast to the 80 seat VRs, May 1970 also saw the arrival of a 16 seat Ford Transit. It had bodywork by Strachan, and was purchased for the Bath tourist service, in place of No. 400, the ex-Silver Star Trojan. The Transit, numbered 401 (XAE 965H), carried pale green livery. To make room for new buses, it was renumbered 300 in 1975, but following the withdrawal of the service, it was sold in 1982.

Allan Macfarlane

Plate 187: Starting with the G-registered batch, dual-purpose RELHs had bodies based on the bus shell *(see Plate 168)*, with extra brightwork and a rear boot. The 1970 batch, Nos. 2059—68 (WHW 371—80H), had narrower, two-leaf entrances, and introduced curved glass windscreens. This is shown by No. 2065, leaving Bath for Frome.

Allan Macfarlane

Plate 188: More RESL 43 seaters arrived during 1970—2, but these had revised chassis dimensions resulting in a different pillar spacing *(see Plate 174).* These buses were particularly associated with Bath over the years, the last departing in 1983, and No. 517 (YHT 803J) is shown at Parade Gardens on route 207.

Dave Withers

Plate 189: While the City fleet was taking large quantities of dual-door RELLs, similar buses for Cheltenham District, Gloucester City and Bath Services continued to be delivered regularly, although in their usual small numbers. Cheltenham District's dark red and cream colours are carried by No. 1202 (YHY 582J) of 1970, although in this view the bus lacks the name Cheltenham beneath the borough arms.

Allan Macfarlane

Plate 190: A completely new basis for the coach fleet made its appearance in 1971. The chassis were Leyland Leopards while the stylish bodywork was by Plaxton, whose one previous representative in the fleet was Foden No. 2200 *(see Plate 88).* The new Plaxton bodies were of the highly-acclaimed 'Panorama Elite II' styling, and carried 47 passengers. Very much NBC standard vehicles, they even carried a new NBC-derived livery. This, in common with other South Western fleets, was white, with a coloured waistband — magenta in Greyhound's case. The bold new lettering can be seen in this view of No. 2160 (BHW 85J); the excellent illustration of a Greyhound could also be seen clearly, if it wasn't for the shadow of the street lamp!

Allan Macfarlane

Plate 191: The other units of the Greyhound fleet were subsequently repainted in white and magenta, but on the oldest coaches, the 1960/1 MWs, it didn't quite come off. This can be judged from this shot of No. 2113 (406 LHT), taken in Wells Road, Bristol.

Dave Withers

Plate 192: By way of experiment, and to compare costs with those of a new bus, Bristol Omnibus Company stripped and extensively rebuilt one of their dwindling LS fleet in 1971. In addition to replacing worn or corroded items, the 5HLW engine was replaced by a 6HLW, the windows were remounted in cream rubber, striplights were installed, the interior retrimmed and reupholstered to match the latest REs, the cab was re-equipped and side by side destination boxes were fitted. The guinea-pig was No. 2844 (PHW 934) of 1953 which, in fact, had been withdrawn from service three times since 1967, but kept bouncing back! It is shown here on a Hanham local, on its second day out, and still with incomplete destination displays. Compare this with *Plate 105*.

Allan Macfarlane

Plate 193: The rebuilding of No. 2844 was considered a success, so seven more were treated over the next year or so. These used 1957 buses as a basis and they also received a restyled front end . . . although the result was not particularly pretty! Rubber-mounted flat windscreens were installed, together with a heavy-looking demister bar, and squarer front domes were fitted. After the second rebuild, the subject being No. 2904 (XHW 420), a new numbering series was introduced — 3000 onwards. No. 3006 (YHY 74), seen here in Marlborough Street in 1974, was formerly No. 2916.

Allan Macfarlane

Plate 194: In May 1971, FLF6B No. C7133 (826 SHW) was experimentally repainted in the double deck one-man-operation livery. One month later, the Tilling green was overpainted in Lincoln Green, using paint in stock while the Company was repainting some ex-South Wales AEC Swifts on behalf of London Country. No. C7133, seen here at Southmead, on route 87 (formerly 8A), retained this scheme until August 1973.

Graham Jones

Plate 195: An FLF that appeared in November 1971 had everybody staring; it was the Company's first overall advertisement! No. C7109 (802 SHW) was the bus, and it was painted dark red and covered with slogans for 'Berni Inns'. The bus is pictured here on route 88 (formerly 8) at Southmead. By the end of 1983, sixty seven more overall adverts had appeared.

Dave Withers

Plate 196: A new lightweight single decker was introduced by Bristol Commercial Vehicles in 1967, termed LH6L when fitted with the Leyland 0.400 engine. Bristol took none until 1972, when six entered service as Nos. 351—356 (DHW 291—6K). They had 43 seats, and were unusual among LHs in having semi-automatic transmission. Their livery differed from other saloons in having no green footing to the skirt panels. Later, a reversing window was fitted to the lower back panel, causing the removal of one seat. They spent virtually all their lives at Weston and Wells, until retired as early as 1979. No. 356 is seen here among the trees at Shepton Mallet.

Allan Macfarlane

Plate 197: With a City RELL fleet of around 130 already in service or on order, the Company at last decided to evaluate some VRTs, and even then, only a mere eight were delivered, in 1972, and were numbered C5002—9 (EHU 361—8K). Their dual-door 70 seat bodies were equipped for one-man-operation, which was, by now, widely accepted on double deckers, so they carried one-man-operation livery. It is believed that the first to enter service were Nos. C5005/6, on 1st April 1972, serving crew-operated routes 88 and 1, respectively. After that, the VRs were not used properly until converting the 22/23 to one-man-operation (with RELL support) on 23rd July. Nos. C5005 and C5008 are seen here, one on each route, at the Lockleaze terminus. Power for these buses was supplied by Gardner 6LXB engines.

Graham Jones

Plate 198: In 1972, Bristol Omnibus took advantage of Western National's decision to reduce its orders in two ways. Firstly, fourteen Gardner-engined RELL6Gs, with standard B44D bodies, were diverted to the City, and secondly, three RELH6Gs, with Plaxton 'Panorama Elite II' C47F bodies, entered the Greyhound fleet as Nos. 2161—3 (EHW 313—5K). They were readily identifiable by their top-mounted destination screens, (known as 'Bristol domes' throughout the trade, even when not on Bristols!), coupled with extra radiator air intakes *(see Plate 190)*. No. 2161 was photographed at Bath.

Allan Macfarlane

Plate 199: Another addition to the Greyhound fleet in 1972 was a two year old 'Panorama Elite' 49 seat Leyland Leopard, also shown at Bath. This, however, was only on hire. It was new, in September 1970, as Rhondda No. 323 (YTX 323H), passing with the Rhondda fleet to Western Welsh in January 1971, as No. 2323. It was renumbered 108 and received their livery in November 1971, but was sold to Greenslades of Exeter, as No. 407, in January 1972, duly receiving their colours . . . only to be hired to Bristol in February, and so gaining Greyhound colours! Two Greenslades RELH6L/Plaxtons, one new in May 1971 to Devon General's Grey Cars, were also hired, and carried Greyhound colours. All were returned to Greenslades by May.

Allan Macfarlane

Plate 200: The start of a new era of NBC standardisation began, early in 1973, with the placing in service of 34 examples of the NBC/Leyland joint venture, the Leyland National. It was a technically sophisticated integral saloon (the LS had been Bristol's only integral vehicle beforehand), and arrived after years of development. Despite that, the early models were beset with problems, aggravated by industrial unrest which meant that spares for anything were in short supply. The National was designed to be the NBC's standard single decker, which meant that the ever-popular (and much more attractively-styled) Bristol RE would eventually be unobtainable. Bristol Omnibus Company's first Leyland Nationals, numbered between C1400 and 1433 (JHU 841—74L), were the first to come in the new NBC livery of leaf green or, for Cheltenham District, poppy red. A thin white line was applied before entering service, and this view of No. C1405 shows the unique fleetname style adopted for City buses. REs and MWs carried the white scroll further back.

Allan Macfarlane

Plate 201: Twenty VRs, which arrived in 1973, also carried leaf green livery and again displayed the unique fleetname style. They were of improved frontal styling, and at last brought the VR total to the same as that cancelled in 1969. The buses completed conversion of the 22/23 to double deck one-man-operation, and turned the 21 over. No. C5015 (LHW 796L) is seen at Lawrence Weston. The 28 'Series 2' VRs have borne the brunt of Muller Road depot's busy duties admirably ever since.

Allan Macfarlane

Plate 202: Repainting the rest of the fleet into NBC shades began late in 1972, although for a while, Bristol Joint Services had special dispensation to retain the gold scroll fleetname and the one-man-operation livery; the latter, however, used leaf green with the cream, which was very smart. The adoption of the new standard styles was not universally well-accepted, especially in Cheltenham, where the dignified dark red and cream gave way to raucous poppy red. At least the town's name was given prominence on the sides now, and the borough arms was enlarged. Gloucester buses received an equivalent style. The oldest buses painted poppy red were KSW6Gs Nos. 8561 and 8562 (UHY 374 and UHY 375), of October 1955. When No. 8562, seen here, was withdrawn in October 1975, it became the only Bristol Group bus to see twenty years' service in unrebuilt condition! *(See also Plate 118).*

Allan Macfarlane

Plate 203 (above): No LSs other than Nos. 3000—7 *(see Plate 193)* received NBC livery, but MWs of all ages were treated. Bath had a sizeable allocation, most of which received the simplified fleetname Bath (only PMT is a shorter NBC fleetname!). This name was only applied to single deckers, as no double deckers retained Bath Services once FLF6B No. 7216 (DHW 986C) was repainted in leaf green, in January 1975. In this view, No. 2974 (986 EHY) can be seen to have alternating vents, which were applied in a second programme, in 1971 *(see Plate 148).*

Dave Withers

Plate 204: The four Leyland Leopards new in 1973 carried a new NBC coach livery of unbroken white, with red and blue National names towards the rear. A very small Bristol fleetname, regrettably with no mention of Greyhound now, eventually appeared over the front wheel arches. The batch was No. 2164—7 (LHU 661/2/4/3L); Mark III Panorama Elite bodies were carried.

Michael Bennett

Plate 205 (above): Under NBC policies, coaches over seven years old were obliged to be painted in 'local coach' (i.e. dual-purpose) colours, and were discouraged from working express routes. Bristol Omnibus Company dutifully painted RELHs Nos. 2115—34 (see Plate 154) in half-green, half-white . . . and continued to thrash them up and down the M4 to London! The NBC relented, and several received all-white livery before being sold to Western National. No. 2118 (864 UAE) takes a more relaxed duty, in this scene, for Bath racegoers.

Dave Withers

Plate 206: Despite the advent of the Leyland National, thirty more RELLs were delivered, all in NBC livery. The final example was No. 1340 (OAE 962M), seen here at Swindon. Future single deck orders had to be for Leyland Nationals, as the RE was no longer available to the NBC. Some newer REs did, however, arrive in Swindon in 1975, these being owned by Thamesdown Transport; it was ironic that this municipality could buy the Bristol RE, yet Bristol Omnibus could not! Nevertheless, Bristol had taken 439 REs between 1963 and 1973!

Allan Macfarlane

Plate 207: Another minibus was delivered in 1973 (see Plate 186). This 17 seater was a Leyland 440EA, bodied by Asco and finished internally to NBC standards. It was purchased for a Gloucester 'Centrebus' service, and numbered G402 (PHU 647M). In 1975 it became No. G301 but in October 1976, it started a shoppers' service from the Grove Park area of Weston-super-Mare, on a flexible route. Now numbered 301, it is seen here at the bus station. Increased demand meant the introduction of regular routes, so No. 301 later inaugurated a service in the Windmill Hill district of inner Bristol, but was again ousted by bigger buses (see Plate 244).

Allan Macfarlane

Plate 208: Bristol Omnibus Company bought a batch of second-hand coaches in 1973. The five 1966 Leyland Leopards came from Southdown (EUF 195/6/8, 201/13D), and carried Plaxton 'Panorama I' C49F bodies. Numbered 2168—72, they initially ran in Southdown's light green livery, but No. 2172 is in National white in this view. They were withdrawn during 1977/8.

Allan Macfarlane

Plate 209: Other second-hand purchases in 1973 were two extra convertible open top Lodekkas. They were 1959 LD6Bs (with BVW engines) from Crosville (626 HFM and 627 HFM), and were numbered L8580 and L8581. They featured polished beading at waist level and platform doors, and entered service in the cream livery with the Weston coat of arms. No. L8580 is seen here with a traditional seaside blackboard advertising its forthcoming tour.

Allan Macfarlane

Plate 210: A third additional open top LD to appear in 1973 was designed as part of the events to celebrate, as it says on the side of the bus, '1373–1973 Bristol 600th Charter Anniversary'. The original date saw the granting of City and County status to Bristol; 1974 was to see Bristol absorbed by the County of Avon! The Lodekka (WHY 947) operated a circular tour of Bristol, taking in the 600 Exhibition on The Downs. New in 1956 as No. L8394, it was rebuilt as shown after sustaining roof damage and was accordingly renumbered L8582. It continued the Bristol Tour each year until 1980.

Allan Macfarlane

Plate 211: Ten of the twelve 1966 dual-purpose MW6Gs *(see Plate 160)* were relegated to stage duties as Nos. 2417–26 as early as 1970, subsequently receiving one-man-operation livery as they came due for a repaint. They retained their coach seats, however, until being recertified in 1973, when they also gained NBC livery. Unfortunately, the forced-air ventilation nozzles didn't line up with their newly-acquired bus seats! The unusual appearance of these buses, with their fixed side windows, is captured by No. 2422 (HAE 266D) at Stroud. The six cylinder engines were a bonus on Stroud's hilly routes.

Allan Macfarlane

Plate 212: The first short length Leyland Nationals, 10.3 metre 44 seaters, arrived late in 1974. They were numbered in the same series as the 11.3 metre examples, as shown here by No. 1454 (GEU 366N) entering Marlborough Street bus station. In June 1975, however, they were renumbered into their own series, starting at 550 (this bus became No. 554). Similarly, 11.3m single-door Nationals started their own series at 3010 (Nos. 3000–7 were still in use on the LS6Gs; *see Plate 193*). Five unfamiliar groups of registration letters, but including FB from Bath, were issued by Bristol Vehicle Licencing Office from October 1974, as shown here.

Allan Macfarlane

Plate 213: In the spring of 1974, following NBC doctrine, the liveries of double deckers not yet repainted leaf green were updated to NBC standards. This meant applying fresh Tilling green paint over the upper cream band and, on the lower panels, over the gold scroll fleetname, the lower cream band was then overpainted in white. Finally, NBC fleetnames were applied. About the same time, fleet numberplates and new depot codes were placed on the front instead of the sides; Lodekkas omitted the L prefix now. The oldest buses given this treatment were 1956 KSW6Gs and LD6Gs (WHW/WHY batches). The oldest Lodekka, Weston's No. 8392 (WHY 933), seen here, shows the patchy effect of the paintwork.

Allan Macfarlane

Plate 214: Updating the one-man-operation livery and Cheltenham District's colours to NBC standards was not possible, so these were generally left alone, apart from receiving the new front-mounted fleet number/depot plates. A few saloons received NBC fleetnames, though, and these were almost exclusively restricted to Stroud buses. Shown here is No. 2403 (926 RAE), a B45F-bodied 1963 MW5G that was previously No. 2022 — *(see Plate 152)*. Incidentally, the last saloons had been repainted, from Tilling green, into one-man-operation livery, only three months before repaints from one-man-operation livery into the NBC scheme started!

Allan Macfarlane

Plate 215: Industrial unrest throughout the country in the early 1970s, including the 'Winter of Discontent' and the three day working week, resulted in an acute shortage of spare parts and new vehicles, a shortage which lingered on until 1976. It meant that operators had to make the best use of what they had in stock. Bristol engine spares were so hard to obtain that the surviving KSW6Bs were withdrawn during 1973, and several BVW engines in FLF6Bs were replaced by Gardner 6LWs. In order to cover vehicles off the road awaiting parts, all sorts of buses in roadworthy condition were kept up to scratch. The most surprising event was when two LD6Bs, which had been driver trainers for twelve to eighteen months, were overhauled, repainted leaf green, and returned to passenger traffic in mid-1975! They were No. C8439 (YHT 932) of 1957, seen here, and No. C8491 (822 CHU) of 1959.

Allan Macfarlane

Plate 216: The Company's first single-door VRTs arrived in 1975. Numbered 5500 onwards, the early ones seated 70. Nos. 5500—3 were on Series 2 chassis, but the rest were Series 3 models with enclosed engines and breather grilles in the rear between-decks panels. The four Series 2 buses were put to work at Weston, where No. 5501 (HTC 727N) is seen on its first day of service, 29th July 1975.

Graham Jones

Plate 217: Just after the Cheltenham District fleet had become entirely poppy red, the unpopular decision was taken, in 1975, to paint their buses green in future. In that summer, two new green short Nationals were placed in the CDTC fleet, which resulted in green LD No. 8567 (YHT 963) being transferred to Bristol Omnibus Company, the first interfleet transfer involving CDTC for 25 years! *(See Plate 87).* The next new green CDTC buses (the borough arms were not carried on the green) were two VRT/SL3/501s, which were their first double deckers for nine years! They were Nos. 5030 and 5031 (JOU 160P and JOU 161P) and No. 5030 is seen here with the later NBC symbol. The Leyland 501 engine that powered some early Series 3s, was derived from the National's 510 unit, but was not a successful motor. In 1982, the Company started replacing 501s with Gardner 6LXBs.

Allan Macfarlane

Plate 218: Having bought only six LHs, namely those which came in 1972 *(see Plate 196),* a surprise of 1975 was a complete change of policy, in which large numbers of LH6Ls were ordered — no fewer than 110 buses, with B43F bodies and manual transmission arrived by 1980! They not only ousted all MWs, but also the ten year old RESLs *(see Plate 174).* Furthermore, new LHs replaced the oldest LHs in the fleet! No. 381, a 1976 bus, and is pictured here, with a twin, at Trowbridge. The registration is KHU 615P . . . KHU 615 was carried by 1947 K5G No. 1506!

Allan Macfarlane

Plate 219: In the spring of 1976, open top Lodekkas Nos. 8576—81 were repainted in special new liveries, representing the colours of the trams that used to operate within the Company's territory at Gloucester, Cheltenham, Swindon, Bath, Bristol and Weston-super-Mare. The buses also depicted something for which the towns were well-known, and were individually named. No. 8577 (867 NHT) is in maroon and white, is dedicated to Swindon Corporation trams, depicts Swindon-built GWR locomotive *City of Truro* and is named *Western Conqueror*. It is seen at Brean Down, on the new open top service 137 from Burnham-on-Sea.

Allan Macfarlane

Plate 220: In June 1976, an open top 1964 FLF6B was added to the Weston fleet. Formerly No. C7148 (841 SHW), it was now numbered 7900 and painted in blue and white 'Bristol tram' livery, illustrating Concorde and named *Western Challenger*. Only five other open top FLFs ran for NBC companies; four with Eastern National and one ex-Alder Valley bus with Southern Vectis — although Crosville converted some FSFs. In this view, No. 7900 picks up passengers outside Weston bus station.

Martin Curtis

Plate 221: The slow demise of the KSW, the last Bristol type in service with a traditional radiator and a conventional chassis, was eventually completed in June 1976, when No. C8374 (WHW 815) of 1956 and C8428 (YHT 924) of 1957 were withdrawn. The utter reliability of these buses was greatly appreciated during the first half of the 1970s *(see Plate 215)*, and the KSWs saw constant service on many gruelling trunk routes in the City. These included, in particular, routes 73 and 74, via the long and congested Gloucester Road. It is on these routes that Nos. C8370 and C8379 (WHW 811 and WHW 820) are seen at the Royal Oak in Horfield, while tackling the journey into town once more.

Allan Macfarlane

Plate 222: Even as the last KSWs were being withdrawn, the surviving LDs were quickly reaching the end of the road. Most of the Country buses were, in traditional fashion, working out their last days on Bristol City routes, joining the remaining City LDs. During 1975, there had been a concerted effort to repaint the remainder of the Tilling green buses, including two dozen LDs, into leaf green. The resultant smartness belied their age . . . and perhaps their condition, because withdrawals continued swiftly, often coming soon after a repaint! Service revisions in the City, in June 1976, not only laid off all but a handful of the final LDs, but eliminated the City's FSFs, and many early FLFs! The last rear loaders of all (excluding open toppers) were No. G8459 (YHT 946), a 1958 H58R-bodied LD6G, and No. G8548 (438 FHW), a 1960 H60RD-bodied FS6G, which were retired from Gloucester in November 1976. In this September 1975 view, two of the repainted LDs, Nos. 8545 and 8546 (435 FHW and 436 FHW), are joined at Henbury by the last KSW to have been built, No. C8431 (YHT 927), which is in its last few days of service.

Graham Jones

Plate 223: After years during which the City fleet was replenished with a large number of 44 seat single deckers (more than 180), yet only 28 seventy seat VRs, it was decided that there was a place for the double decker in Bristol after all. Nearly fifty VRs arrived in 1976, many being placed at Staple Hill depot for routes 52—55. Seen here is No. C5047 (LEU 255P) leaving Blackhorse, near Downend, on route 52 when still crew-operated. As it happened, agreement could not be reached on one-manning Staple Hill's network of services, on the edge of the City, so the 52—55 went one-man-operated using single deckers. The VRs were used instead to convert other City routes to double deck one-man-operation.

Graham Jones

Plate 224: On rare occasions, Bristol Omnibus Company has exchanged buses with other operators for short spells. In recent times, this is usually to enable an overall advertisement to be seen more widely. Such an occasion saw a Devon General VRT/SL3/6LXB working in Bristol. It was their No. 571 (MOD 571P), advertising Tesco Supermarkets, and is seen at the White Tree in May 1977. It returned the next year, by which time the reference to Green Shield Stamps had been deleted following their removal from circulation. Twice, while Bristol overall advertisements have gone south, green Western National VRs have worked in the City.

Allan Macfarlane

Plate 225: The country went to town in 1977, to celebrate the Silver Jubilee of Her Majesty Queen Elizabeth II. Bristol Omnibus Company's main contribution was the repainting of three buses in silver livery with a blue band, together with the Jubilee lettering and emblem. The Jubilee buses were an FLF, a VR and a new Leyland National, NWS 903R, which had appeared in silver the previous September at the Commercial Motor Show. Although this B44D-bodied bus was officially City stock, numbered C1456, it spent most of the year at Cheltenham or, as shown here, at Gloucester; the C prefix had even been removed by this time.

Allan Macfarlane

Plate 226: The FLF that received Silver Jubilee livery was No. C7312 (KHW 304E), a ten year old FLF6B. Its usual haunt was the 77/78/79 circuit, as shown here at Hartcliffe. The VR, incidentally, was No. 5512 (LHT 722P), which visited various towns in the Company's territory.

Martin Curtis

Plate 227: Since its introduction, the Bath fleetname had been carried by only one group of new buses, five JHU—L Nationals. The withdrawal of MWs, and reallocation of various saloons, reduced its numbers a little, then from the end of 1976, it was discontinued on repainted buses. Added to that was the fact that many of Bath's dual-door RELLs were transferred to Hanham from 1975, to work local services on Bristol's eastern borders, outside the BJS area. The Bath fleetname then quickly diminished, eventually disappearing in 1979, in favour of the Bristol name. Here No. 1197 (YHU 517J), one of their 1970 batch of six B44D-bodied RELL6Ls, passes Parade Gardens in 1978 *(see Plate 7).*

Allan Macfarlane

Plate 228: The initial popularity of two door buses for urban work had faded by the mid-1970s, except in the City. Two doorways continued to be specified, for a while, on VRs, but Leyland Nationals, in B52F form, were added to the local fleets. Seen here is Cheltenham District's No. 3047 (PHW 989S). This is another case of a 'repeated' registration *(see Plate 218)*, but of greater coincidence, as PHW 989 was also a Cheltenham District bus . . . KSW 86! As it happened, only one more new bus arrived with Cheltenham fleetnames, this being No. 3061 (TAE 643S) in 1978. Subsequently, new and repainted buses carried Bristol names and sadly, legal lettering. Indeed, in 1980, the Cheltenham District Traction Company ceased to trade, thirty years after passing to Bristol control.

Allan Macfarlane

Plate 229: Gloucester's first eight dual-door VRs failed to carry the City's crest, simply because there was no room on the nearside between the doors. Nos. G5119—21 (REU 309—11S) of 1977 rectified the situation, with a new scheme that was later applied to the other eight, whereby the name and arms were placed on the leading between-decks panels. This can be seen on No. G5121, as it stops outside the Bristol Hotel.

Allan Macfarlane

Plate 230: The NBC stated that the LH model, together with other lightweights, should only have a life of seven years with their member companies. Alder Valley was one of relatively few companies to comply with this ruling . . . and Bristol was one of many to benefit from their obedience! In February 1977, five LH6Ls with B41F bodies, new during 1969/1970, were acquired and numbered 346—350, in front of the previous oldest. All had flat windscreens, while No. 346 (VMO 227H) was only 7ft. 10in. wide. Featured in this view is No. 349 (AMO 236J), leaving Gloucester bus station for Upton St. Leonards. The five lasted a little over two years with Bristol Omnibus Company.

Allan Macfarlane

Plate 231: The six 1968 Greyhound RELH6Ls, Nos. 2151—6 (NHW 308—13F), were built to 'dual-purpose' specification, with the intention of eventually being relegated *(see Plate 168)*. Their time came during 1975/6, when they received half-green, half-white livery, and were renumbered 2079—84. However, they tended to work frequent reliefs on coach services and due to the NBC being unhappy about dual-purpose liveried vehicles appearing at Victoria, the six were returned to all-white National livery in 1977. They did not revert to their coach numbers, though. No. 2080 (NHW 309F), sparkling in white, speeds through Bristol, but on a bus service for Weston! The vehicles again received green and white in 1979.

Allan Macfarlane

Plate 232: New coaches during 1976—8 had Plaxton's 'Supreme Express' 49 seat coachwork on the Leyland Leopard chassis, and qualified for the bus grant made by the Government towards the purchase price, providing the vehicles were suitable for and occasionally used on stage work. With effect from the M-registered 'Elites', the top destination box had become standard *(see Plates 190 & 198)*. No. 2189 (ROU 347S) stands with its power doors open at Bath depot.

Allan Macfarlane

Plate 233: On 15th July 1978, Bristol Joint Services ceased to exist. The agreement between Bristol Corporation and the Company, that had been in existence since 1937, was terminated, leaving the Company entirely responsible for the City's bus services. New City buses since 1976, and repainted buses since 1977, had carried 'Country' names in anticipation *(see Plate 223)*, but it was to be December 1979 before the white scroll and crest disappeared. Here, No. C1321 (MHW 281L) demonstrates the most distinctive City fleetname of all time. After the ending of Bristol Joint Services, the C prefix was deleted, and there was no limitation on the use of Country buses working on City routes *(see Plate 48)*. Eventually, some services were revised and extended beyond the bounds of the old Bristol Joint Services area, particularly in the Hanham/Kingswood district, benefiting residents of those parts with more useful routes into Bristol.

Allan Macfarlane

Plate 234: Leyland National developed an 'economy' version of the short model, in 1978, called the B series. It was intended that the Bristol LH would thereby cease production, but Bristol Omnibus Company succeeded in taking both types! The fifteen B Nationals were numbered 700—714 and the first, VAE 499T, is pictured here leaving Swindon bus station. The unsightly houses in the background were eventually demolished to make way for new developments, including a new bus station, in the 1980s. Note the National's reduced ventilating, the lack of roof pod and the plainer front, compared with previous Nationals.

Allan Macfarlane

Plate 235: For new services in the valleys around Nailsworth, introduced to replace some that the last SUSs and, once, Bedford OBs and even Western National had operated, Bristol Omnibus Company bought two Ford Transits, with Reeve-Burgess bodies, containing 17 coach seats. They were Nos. 302 and 303 (VFB 188T and VFB 189T), and were painted green and yellow. Gloucestershire County Council financially supported the services, and their crest can be seen on the side of No. 303 which is pictured at Nailsworth bus station.

Allan Macfarlane

Plate 236: Reorganisation of the operation of coach services in 1978, in association with National Travel (South West), meant that Bristol Omnibus Company's coach fleet was largely made redundant. The entire fleet of thirty had Plaxton bodies and all were Leopards, with the exception of three RELH6Gs *(see Plate 114).* Six were then sold to National Travel, Nos. 2176—81 (RHY 764—9M), while the oldest nine were stored for gradual conversion to one-man-operation. They returned to service one by one during 1979, renumbered 2085—93 and painted green and white (except Nos. 2092 and 2093, which remained white for reliefs from Swindon on the M4 services). No. 2085 (YHU 521J), formerly No. 2157, demonstrates the adapted destination display. The vehicles were not successful on stage, though, so withdrawals began about a year later; indeed, conversion of No. 2091, an RELH, was never completed and it was sold. The fifteen Leopards that were kept as coaches were renumbered 2300—14, in April 1979.

Allan Macfarlane

Plate 237: The relegation of the Leopard coaches to dual-purpose status caused the earliest dual-purpose vehicles to assume bus status, in the usual manner. This time, though, it was the first turn for the RELHs, which were renumbered from 2041—9 to 2436—44 and repainted in bus livery — in which they looked odd — although they retained their coach seats. *(See Plate 168).* Seen here is No. 2442 (KHW 316E).

Allan Macfarlane

Plate 238 (above): Another case of 'one of those things' concerning Lodekka grilles involved former City FLF6B No. 7253 (FHW 158D) which, between September 1979 and February 1982, carried the original pre-1962 type of cowl. Two other FLFs had similar cowls over the years. In this view, No. 7253 passes through Pucklechurch, on one of Staple Hill depot's out-of-town school runs *(see Plate 223)*.

Allan Macfarlane

Plate 239: The Leyland National 2 was introduced in 1980, in place of the original model. Its engine was the L11 unit, derived from the O.680 as used in Bristol's REs, and it had a front radiator which produced a bulbous snout. Bristol Omnibus Company ordered fifty of B specification *(see Plate 234)*, with which it was intended to eliminate all remaining crew-operated double deckers outside Bristol City. This almost completed the Company's plans for predominantly single deck operation (no Country VRs had arrived since 1978). There was some opposition to this within the Company, but for all that, the first National 2s replaced the last FLFs at Cheltenham, as well as on the Bristol to Bath trunk. No. 3507 (AAE 651V) works a Cheltenham town service in this view. The white band was first extended around the front of the Nationals on the VEU—T batch of 11351A/1Rs.

Dave Russell and Deric Pemberton

Plate 240: The last LH6Ls entered service in the summer of 1980, on the very last LH chassis to be built. The final delivery consisted of Nos. 454—466 (AFB 585—97V), with Bristol and United Auto alone taking V-registered LHs new, and bringing the total delivered since 1975 to 110 *(see Plate 218)*. They were allocated to depots throughout the Company's area, particularly Stroud and Gloucester, yet Cheltenham had few. It is at Cheltenham that No. 463 is shown in this picture.

Allan Macfarlane

Plate 241: The last 23 new dual-door VRs (Bristol City still insisted on this layout) appeared in May and June 1980, numbered 5135—5157 (AHU 512—23V and AHW 198—208V). These buses had several new features, such as Widney ventilators — note the long hoppers — square side and tail-light clusters, and a cab heater, which needed a breather grille behind the driver's window. These were the first buses to have fully-automatic transmission. No. 5138 stands in Crow Lane, Henbury — compare with *Plate 56*. The 77/78 was still crew worked, and although this was the third time it had been furnished with new VRs, it soon reverted to 100 per cent FLF operation!

Allan Macfarlane

Plate 242: Bristol Omnibus was one of three NBC firms that received a new breed of bus, the MCW Metrobus (Maidstone & District and Northern General were the others). Both chassis and 76 seat body were built by the well-known body building consortium Metro-Cammell Weymann *(see Plates 83 and 84)*. It is said that the Metrobus was introduced to counter Leyland's dominance and ever more restricted range. Bristol Omnibus Company specified Rolls-Royce Eagle 220 engines, despite the availability of the 6LXB, and they had Voith fully-automatic transmission. The five Metrobuses were numbered 6000—4 (DAE 510—4W; DAE 510—4K were carried by RELLs), and all entered service in Bath with special liveries. These promoted the Company's concessionary fare schemes, and featured a yellow front, with the rest of the bus another colour — red, blue, green, orange and yellow, respectively. No. 6003, seen here, received standard leaf green in 1983. It shows well the characteristic asymmetrical windscreens.

Allan Macfarlane

Plate 243: The summer of 1980 saw the appearance of the first rear-engined open toppers in the fleet. In 1979 four 1967 Leyland Atlantean PDR1/2s, with Roe bodies, were bought for conversion to open top, from Hants & Dorset, who had acquired them with the fleet of 'King Alfred' of Winchester in 1973. Bristol Omnibus Company numbered them 8600—3 (HOR 592/1/0/89E) but, in the event, No. 8601 was never converted, and was scrapped. No. 8600 did trial service in October 1979, in all-cream livery, but the three had green waistbands for 1980/1. They enabled Lodekkas Nos. 8579—81 and K5G No. 8583 to be retired. No. 8603 does little business on this wet May day. Note the enlarged side window, to improve the driver's vision.

Allan Macfarlane

Plate 244: The Windmill Hill Community bus, otherwise known as Asco-bodied Leyland 440EA No. 301 *(see Plate 207),* was soon found to be too small for the job, and Bristol Omnibus Company borrowed a Marshall-bodied LHS (26ft. by 7ft. 6in.) and a brand-new LHS/ECW (25ft. 9in. by 7ft. 6in.) from Western National, to try on the roads. They were successful, so two B35F-bodied LHS6Ls were bought, in 1980, from London Country. These, however, were 26ft. 6in. by 8ft. but, nevertheless, Nos. 304 and 305 (RPH 105L and RPH 108L) presented no serious problems. They were new in 1972, and one was kept as spare bus. No. 305, arriving at The Centre, on one of its few journeys beyond Bedminster, displays the special livery applied to the pair in 1983.

Allan Macfarlane

Plate 245:   October 1980 saw the first massive shake-up in bus services implemented in accordance with the 'Market Analysis Project'. This was a thorough survey on passenger demands, operational costings, etc., made by an independent team for the NBC. For the enthusiast, the results were grim (very often grim, too, for passengers in wayward places) as large numbers of buses were declared surplus as routes were trimmed or even closed completely, but something had to be done to curb the bus industry's collapsing financial state, and to reflect present day travel habits; as it was, MAP came out strongly in favour of double deckers, which contradicted Bristol Omnibus Company's policy *(see Plate 239)*. As a result, the last fifteen of the fifty Leyland National 2s were cancelled, and London Country was found willing to sell its entire VR fleet of just fifteen buses, which were new in 1977. These had Leyland 501 engines, and their bodies were to the maximum height of 14ft. 6in. (13ft. 8in. was Bristol Omnibus Company's norm). They were, therefore, afforded their own numbering series, 6500—14 (PPH 461—75R). The first buses, complete with Grays and Tilbury area adverts, were pressed into service in December 1980 and January 1981. No. 6502 was one of the more thorough overhauls and is seen in Clevedon, one of the areas to witness the return of double deckers after many years' absence.

Allan Macfarlane

Plate 246:   The year 1981 brought the surprising entry into service of more second-hand double deckers . . . three 1968 Northern Counties-bodied Daimler Fleetlines! Together with Nos. 8605 and 8606 *(see Plate 252)*, they were the first Daimlers in the fleet, and the first NCME bodies since the acquisition of No. 3782 in 1950 *(see Plate 75)*. They came from City of Oxford (KFC 372—4G). Bristol Omnibus Company numbered them 7000—2 (despite many FLFs still occupying the 7000s) and, after overhaul, they entered service at Weston. Their rather heavy steering and unfamiliar features made them unpopular and they were withdrawn, for spares, early in 1982. In April 1982, however, No. 7000 was reinstated, but for exclusive use on Bristol's Studentlink service 18, between the Stoke Bishop Halls and the University. It is seen on The Downs in this view. No. 7000 ran for the last time, at the end of term, in June.

Allan Macfarlane

Plate 247: MAP's emphasis on double deckers resulted in the diversion of nineteen new VRs to Bristol, in 1981, for Country services, their first since early 1978. They were surplus to Hants & Dorset's requirements (due to MAP again), and were numbered 5528—46, their engines being unusual in that they were Leyland 680 units. The reason for these being fitted was that industrial problems had caused a shortage of Gardner 6LXBs; Bristol Omnibus Company and Southdown alone agreed to take 680 engines. Despite being a better motor than the 501 *(see Plate 217)*, the Company started replacing 680s by 6LXBs in 1983. No. 5538 (EWS 746W) was one of six placed at Stroud which, prior to the MAP changes, had possessed only one double decker, No. 5512, and that ventured out at peak times only.

Allan Macfarlane

Plate 248: The new and second-hand VRs helped a good deal to extend one-man-operated double deck operation to Country services, but still there were not sufficient numbers and, therefore, several withdrawn FLFs were reinstated in Bristol to enable dual-door VRs to move to other locations. Even after the City services had been recast in October 1981, following MAP, two man operation using FLFs was retained on the 74/75 (now cross-City), 77/78 and 87/88 services. All 64 of Bristol Omnibus Company's FLFs were now shared by the three surviving City depots; Lawrence Hill, Muller Road and Winterstoke Road. Some quite elderly buses were to be found, and many received light overhauls and repaints to keep them smart. The reduction in this fleet was only gradual, which meant that No. 7122 (815 SHW), a former Gloucester 1963 FLF6G, almost became the second bus in the Company's history to see twenty years' service without rebuilding! *(See Plate 202).*

Allan Macfarlane

Plate 249: The retention of the FLFs, the reallocation of dual-door VRs and the arrival of additional VRs was the interesting and beneficial aspect of MAP. On the other hand, its effects on the current single deck fleet was devastating. Any single decker with a low seating capacity was a subject for withdrawal, irrespective of age. B43F LH6Ls went by the dozen, some after as little as eighteen months' service (Hants & Dorset bought no fewer than 42 of the newer ones, which saved some P-registered examples . . . for a while). Several 45, 47 and 49 seat dual-purpose RELHs were sold, rather than being demoted to buses, and all the bus-liveried ones were sold too. Then there were the B44D RELLs; these were withdrawn by the score, some after only nine years' service, and all B44D Leyland Nationals were transferred to Bristol City to see off more RELLs. It transformed places like The Centre in Bristol, where scenes like this, with six RELLs fighting for kerbside space, disappeared overnight. After January 1982, the remaining dual-door saloons — RELLs and Leyland Nationals — were only to be found in Bristol.

Allan Macfarlane

Plate 250: During 1980, to meet a call for increased seating capacity, the Company rebuilt two Cheltenham dual-door Leyland Nationals, Nos. 1432 and 1433 (JHU 873L and JHU 874L), to B52F, and renumbered them 3083 and 3084. Following this successful move, during 1981/2, they rebuilt sixteen of the surplus dual-door RELLs to B50F — an exact reversal of trends twelve years earlier! *(See Plate 178).* Surprisingly, in view of the number of late model RELLs available for rebuilding, five flat screen WAE—H buses were treated. The oldest was No. 1157 (WAE 790H), seen here in Bath. The only sign of them having had a centre door is that the three rows of ventilation slots, below the waistband, are in the third bay instead of the fourth.

Allan Macfarlane

Plate 251: Entering service at Weston, in 1981, was another open topped second-hand Leyland Atlantean. This was a 1963 machine with Weymann body (612 UKM) and came from Maidstone & District back in January 1980. It was numbered 8604, and is seen at the Old Pier.

Martin Curtis

Plate 252: Two other second-hand buses, bought for open top conversion, were ex-Midland Red 1967 Daimler Fleetline CRG6LXs Nos. 8605 and 8606 (LHA 623F and LHA 615F). They had Alexander bodywork which was yet another 'new' make to the fleet. The former managed to see service before the end of the 1980 season, No. 8606 appearing in 1981. Due to their purchase, the last open top Lodekkas, No. 8576—8, were retired after the summer of 1980, although No. 8578 came back for a further season in 1981 — the last rear entrance bus to run for Bristol Omnibus Company. This view shows the one-man-operated open top fleet of 1981, with Nos. 8606 and 8605 leading Nos. 8604/3/2/0!

Martin Curtis

Plate 253: Although the demoted Leopard/Plaxton coaches were not successful on stage duties *(see Plate 236)* the two RELHs, Nos. 2089 and 2090 (EHW 313K and EHW 314K) faired better — which is ironical, seeing that No. 2091 (EHW 315K) was sold before conversion! Indeed, a special duty was found for No. 2090. It emerged from overhaul, in April 1981, with promotional lettering on the sides for the Bristol to Cardiff route *(see Plate 160)*, now renumbered X10. It is seen on these duties at the top of Blackboy Hill. Six months later No. 2090 was repainted again, this time in white with 'Expresswest' red and blue striped logos along the sides, for the revised X10—X12 service running beyond Cardiff to Swansea and West Wales. Unfortunately, the new schedules required a faster vehicle, so No. 2090 returned to a more flexible role in June 1982, this time painted white with a green waistband *(see Plate 254)*. She was withdrawn, however, in November 1983.

Allan Macfarlane

Plate 254: The remaining 'Elite' coaches, Nos. 2300—6 (LHU 661/3L, RHY 761—3/70/1M), were sold to National Travel in 1980, then in June 1981 'Supremes' Nos. 2311 and 2312 received green waistbands, followed in July by all eight, Nos. 2307—14, being reclassified as dual-purpose and renumbered 2094—2101. All received this smart new scheme of white with a green waistband, as exemplified by No. 2095 (LEU 272P) passing through Bath. Nos. 2096 and 2100 carried promotional lettering on this livery, for the Bristol to Gloucester service 820, emphasising the return fare of £1.95.

Allan Macfarlane

Plate 255: Production of the Bristol VR ceased in August 1981, after which Bristol Commercial Vehicles commenced full production of the Leyland-badged Olympian. This new chassis was designed by Bristol, together with their 'Governors' Leyland, as the successor to the VR, the Daimler Fleetline and the Leyland Atlantean. Bristol Omnibus Company took thirty Gardner-powered ONLXB/1Rs in 1982, with bodywork of standard Olympian styling, which was built, not by ECW, but by Roe — among NBC firms, only London Country was also to choose Roe. The interior styling of these bodies, (whether Roe or ECW) was not to the quality Bristol had been used to over the previous thirty years, with the Olympian's angular coving, square corners and grime-attracting rims to the windows. Seating was H47/29F, in a bus 14ft. 2in. high. The windscreen was the traditional attractive Roe shape — indeed, the same as in the 1967 open toppers Nos. 8600—3! Numbered 9500 upwards — the highest numbers ever used — several were delivered in white, only to receive green before entering service. It was November 1982 before the reasons became clear . . . seven were to run 'limited stop' Bristol City services, the first time single-door one-man-operated double deckers had appeared in the City. Avon County was sponsoring the routes and they were promoted as 'Clipper' buses, finished in white, with Kingfisher and pale blue bands round the lower panels, and Sea Stags (ACC's emblem) on the front. No. 9502 (JHU 901X), seen here on the X68, was joined by Nos. 9504/15/26—9. Their green cousins ran country and town services throughout the Company's area.

Allan Macfarlane

Plate 256: When Southdown withdrew ten of their 1972 dual-door VRT/SL6Gs, Bristol Omnibus Company snapped them up for City services and numbered them 5200—9 (WUF 527—30/2—7K). They were similar to No. 5002—9 *(see Plate 197)*, but had large, single glass destination screens and green moquette on the seats. No. 5203 is shown at Avonmouth, just after entering service in June 1982.

Allan Macfarlane

Plate 257: Further route revision at Swindon, at the end of 1982, resulted in a new fleetname appearing — Swindon and District. It is carried here by No. 5049 (LEU 257P), one of the dual-door VRs transferred from Bristol during MAP. It is working one of the revised services on which the 400 prefix was dropped, returning the numbers to something like their traditional series. Earlier in 1982, the fleetname Cheltenham reappeared after 18 months' absence . . . and, in a far more extensive form, being applied to all that depot's buses! At the same time, all Gloucester depot's country buses gained Gloucester (without the coat of arms). These were the first moves towards a more localised management.

Allan Macfarlane

Plate 258: An increase in express work led Bristol Omnibus Company to acquire two 1973 Leyland Leopard/Plaxton 'Elite III' coaches in 1982, . . . these being generally similar to those sold in 1980! They came from Midland Red, and were numbered 2102 and 2103 (HHA 197L and HHA 198L). There were only 44 seats in these vehicles, which retained an all-white livery, with red Swindon and District fleetnames. No. 2103 is shown in Bristol. A more interesting 1973 coach was bought in May 1983, an RELH6G, with 'Elite III' coachwork (XOO 877L). This, too, was placed at Swindon, and it was most fitting that the fleet number chosen was 2091 — the number allocated to but never carried by the third of Bristol's own RELH6G/Plaxtons *(see Plate 236)*. The 'new' No. 2091 came from Eastern National.

Allan Macfarlane

Plate 259: The Company's ever increasing involvement in express services *(see Plate 258)* led them to refurbish the 1972 dual-purpose RELH6Ls Nos. 2069—78 (GHY 131—40K), the last dual-purpose buses to be delivered. In 1982 they gained new flooring, new upholstery, and a smart new livery of white, with green window surrounds and waistband. Their attractive appearance can be judged from No. 2072, pictured entering Marlborough Street from a short Country route.

Allan Macfarlane

Plate 260: Despite the additional coaches placed at Swindon, staff there had a soft spot for their ageing dual-purpose RELH6Ls and, in particular, for the two surviving coach pattern 1968 machines, Nos. 2079 and 2083 (NHW 308F and NHW 312F), the only examples to live through MAP. The two came into their own during the long rail strike in the summer of 1982. Even afterwards, they could be found on some long cross-country coach routes, as shown here by No. 2079, which is passing through Bath on the 747 from Bristol, continuing to Swindon, Oxford, Northampton, Bedford, Cambridge and Norwich! Of course the vehicle was new as a Greyhound coach (No. 2151) and obviously long-distance travel was still in its blood.

Allan Macfarlane

Plate 261: The pressure on the 'coach' fleet resulted in two Leyland Leopards being hired from East Midland, between November 1982 and January 1983. Numbered 2 and 3 (NNN 2M and NNN 3M), they had Duple Dominant C49F bodies which were a new shape for the Company. In this view, No. 2 leaves Bristol on 'Express' 772.

Allan Macfarlane

Plate 262: Weston's open toppers appeared in a new livery for 1982 — white, with a light blue skirt, adorned by the name 'Coast Rider'. No. 8603 is seen here, in 1983, on the new through service, combining the Weston seafront route with the Brean Down to Burnham-on-Sea service *(see Plate 219).*

Allan Macfarlane

Plate 263: The first single door one-man-operated double deckers for general use on Bristol City routes, were fourteen Olympians, which took over from FLFs on the 87 in July 1983 (route 88 remained in the hands of FLFs). Here, No. 9538 (NTC 137Y) negotiates the White Tree roundabout, while on its way to Filton. By the time these Olympians were built at Brislington, the Bristol Commercial Vehicles factory was under sentence of death. The NBC had withdrawn its share in the manufacturing companies at the end of 1982, leaving Leyland as sole owners of Bristol Commercial Vehicles. Then, in January 1983, and with almost indecent haste, Leyland announced that the closure of Bristol Commercial Vehicles would take place in October of the same year which, coincidentally, saw the 75th Anniversary of the building of the first 'Bristol'! Bristol Omnibus Company received one more batch of 'Bristol' Olympians, in December 1983; Nos. 9545—54 (A945—954 SAE).

Allan Macfarlane

Plate 264: A move to buying coaches again, saw the arrival in 1983 of fifteen examples of a new breed; Leyland Tigers, with Plaxton's excellent 'Paramount 3200' coachwork. They were the first 12 metre vehicles in the fleet, carrying 53 passengers, and starting a new numbering series of 2200—2214 — reflections of the 1937 coaches *(see Plate 8)*. Seen here leaving Marlbrough Street is No. 2204 (A204 RHT), carrying the new National Express livery, with red and blue stripes. Note that from this point, the Company aimed to match fleet and registration numbers. A similar 49 seat Paramount body was built, in 1983, on the Leopard chassis of No. 2098 (PWS 492S), after the original had been burnt out. It was the first example of new bodywork on an older chassis since 1951!

Allan Macfarlane

Plate 265: The new National Express livery shown in *Plate 264* was joined by a series of similarly styled schemes for 'local coach' vehicles. There was a seemingly endless choice of colours, but the application was always the same, with a coloured waistband blended with a diagonal band of dual-coloured stripes behind the front wheels, and dual-coloured stripes around the front. This produced a unique identity for the operator and, at the same time, an NBC Corporate Identity — equally as important. Bristol chose the colours of kingfisher blue and light blue, as demonstrated here by No. 2097 (PWS 491S). Compare this with *Plates 232 and 254*. Sadly, this particular livery was short-lived, as National Express colours were applied for 1984.

Allan Macfarlane

Plate 266: During 1982, the NBC instigated the transfer of middle-aged VRs from company to company. The firms who provided the VRs (a) had a high fleet content of one-man-operable double deckers and (b) were taking new double deckers into stock. The recipients were firms who needed extra or replacement one-man-operated double deckers. Bristol Omnibus Company qualified to receive some 'Cascaded' VRs, as they were termed, due to the number of single deckers and two-man-operated FLFs still in stock. In 1982/3, therefore, thirteen VRT/SL6Gs of 1974/5 vintage and four 1975 VRT/SL3/6LXs arrived. They came from East Midland, United Auto and West Riding, and were numbered 5600—5616 (JNU 136—9N, HPT 82—6N, GUA 381—4N and MUA 872—5P). All had single doorways. They were all overhauled and repainted before going on the road, except for ex-United No. 5606, which went straight to Swindon in poppy red, and with the United name clearly visible on the nearside! It is shown here on local route 2, one of the small number of Thamesdown Transport services now being run jointly with Bristol Omnibus Company. Swindon was to receive eight of the 'Cascaded' buses, to enable dual-door VRs to return to Bristol from whence FLFs were withdrawn.

Allan Macfarlane

Plate 267: The former West Riding Series 2 buses, Nos. 5609—12 (GUA 381—4N), were the oldest of the seventeen 'Cascaded' VRs, dating from 1974. They were readily distinguishable because their windows were mounted in grey rubber, in the same manner as Nos. 5010—29 *(see Plate 201).* Furthermore, they carried the larger destination screens as fitted to the ex-Southdown VRs Nos. 5200—9 *(see Plate 256).* Swindon & District received all four of these buses, and No. 5612 was also photographed while working route 2.

Dave Withers

Plate 268: West Riding supplied the only Series 3s to pass to Bristol at this time, namely Nos. 5613—6 (MUA 872—5P) and once again the buses featured the large destination screens, offering immediate recognition. No. 5614, seen here on Bristol's Centre, was one of only two 'Cascaded' VRs to be allocated to Marlborough Street. Drivers found the 6LX engines in all the acquired VRs to be a little sluggish, compared with the 6LXBs with which they were familiar.

Allan Macfarlane

Plate 269: In April 1983, a new 'limited stop' service was introduced between Bristol, Bath and Salisbury. Numbered X41, it absorbed the 241 between Trowbridge and Salisbury, a route which was once jointly run by Western National and Wilts & Dorset. From the early 1970s, though, it was Bristol Omnibus and Hants & Dorset who ran the 241. The X41 retained the joint operation, but the Wilts & Dorset name was resurrected just a few days before the X41 was introduced. To work the service, five Leyland National 2s, Nos. 3518—20 (AAE 662—4V) and Nos. 3532 and 3533 (BOU 7V and BOU 8V), were reseated to DP49F by Willowbrook in Loughborough, and repainted in dual-purpose livery. No. 3518, pictured at Bath, works the hourly Warminster service, as only every other hour was Salisbury reached.

Dave Withers

Plate 270: Two other second-hand VRs to enter the fleet, in 1983, were convertible open top buses with a history. They were part of a batch of six delivered in late 1977 to Hants & Dorset as Nos. 3374—9 (UFX 855—60S), shortly before service revisions, in conjunction with Bournemouth Transport, deprived Hants & Dorset of its open top routes! In 1979, therefore, the six were swapped for standard VRs from Southern Vectis, the UFXs becoming Nos. 705—710 on the Isle of Wight. Then, in 1983, Vectis agreed to let Bristol have UFX 859S and UFX 860S, but again in exchange for standard VRs. Bristol numbered them 8607 and 8608, and duly despatched Nos. 5524 and 5525 (RFB 614S and RFB 615S) to Vectis. These open toppers were needed for Weston's increased schedules, coupled with the introduction of the Sand Bay—Weston—Burnham-on-Sea route *(see Plate 262)*. No. 8607 leaves Weston bus station here on a lightly laden tea-time journey, and shows the green and white Southern Vectis livery they retained for their one season at Weston before moving to Bath *(see Plate 271)*.

Allan Macfarlane

Plate 271: July and August 1983 saw hot weather and sun in plenty, and in addition to the Weston and Burnham open top service, which was doing so well, Bristol Omnibus Company started an open top Tour of Bath, using Atlantean No. 8600 in all-white. Soon, a duplicate was needed, and Devon General came to the rescue with their No. 935 (VDV 135S), named *Triumph*. This poppy red and white bus was a VRT/SL3/6LXB, identical to Nos. 8607 and 8608 *(see Plate 270)*, and is seen here at Parade Gardens.

Allan Macfarlane

Plate 272: When the Midland Red firm was broken down into five individual self-standing companies, it was found that local control assisted with the running of the businesses. In fact, local control was so effective that the NBC extended the principle to the firms in the West of England in 1983, affecting Western National in January, Hants & Dorset in April and Bristol in September. On 11th September 1983, the Cheltenham & Gloucester Omnibus Co. Ltd., took over from Bristol Omnibus Company in the Gloucester, Cheltenham, Stroud and Swindon areas. There was still a link between the two firms, and no major changes occurred to the fleet. The Central Repair Works at Lawrence Hill was established as Bristol Engineering Ltd. However, in November, it was announced that the new liveries and fleetnames were being adopted for the Cheltenham & Gloucester fleet. The most startling was that Gloucester's allocation was to receive a livery of blue, seldom used in NBC days and each time short-lived. The new fleetname, irrespective of the vehicles' use, was City of Gloucester with the borough arms, the latter being placed on a white base. Demonstrating the new style is No. 3084 (JHU 874L), a former dual-door CDTC Leyland National *(see Plate 250).*

Dave Russell and Deric Pemberton

Plate 273: The new image for Cheltenham-based buses actually had a hint of the old days, as it meant a return to poppy red livery, which was previously applied during 1973/4, although none of Cheltenham's current allocation had ever been in red. It also saw the resumption of the fleetname Cheltenham District, which had not been carried on NBC shades or even on one-man-operated liveried single deckers. It was planned that the borough arms should return as well, and these would be placed on a white base as at Gloucester. Red-liveried No. 5087 (NHU 670R), an H70D-bodied VRT/SL3/6LXB, has yet to receive the arms in this view at the Rotunda; note that, following Swindon's lead, the 500 prefix has gone from the route numbers. The Swindon buses, too, began to receive poppy red livery, while retaining the Swindon and District fleetname.

Dave Russell and Deric Pemberton

Plate 274: It was decided that the Cheltenham & Gloucester buses at Stroud would not change their colours and would remain in leaf green, considered more suitable for the splendid Cotswold countryside. However, a new fleetname appeared, namely Stroud Valleys. This is shown well by No. 5540 (EWS 748W), one of their VRT/SL3/680s, which is seen at Nailsworth. The 'Unibus' pattern of advertising was a popular feature throughout the NBC.

Dave Russell and Deric Pemberton

Plate 275: For their coaching fleet, Cheltenham & Gloucester adopted the separate fleetname of Cotswold, while their 'local coach' livery was white with a leaf green waistband, blended with poppy red bands at the front. This is excellently portrayed by No. 2089 (EHW 313K), one of the RELH6Gs, *(see Plates 198, 236, 253 and 258).* It is shown here about to leave Cheltenham on the X26 for Bath, a regular turn for this coach.

Dave Russell and Deric Pemberton

Plate 276: Later in November 1983, the somewhat reduced Bristol Omnibus Company launched their own series of new fleetnames, each with a local flavour. There were no changes of colour for this company, though. The simple fleetname Bristol became extinct under the new set-up, although the word remained as part of the new identity for buses working Country services out of Bristol, now labelled — as shown here — Bristol Country Bus (coaches were worded Bristol Country). No. 1286 (EHU 383K) was one of only 51 Country RELLs and fourteen dual-door versions in service at the time; Cheltenham & Gloucester inherited eleven RELLs, ten of which ran at Stroud.

Allan Macfarlane

Plate 277: Buses at both Wells and Weston-super-Mare depots gained the fleetname Weston and Wells. Although lacking the double-N motif in this instance, the new name is carried here by No. 5035 (JHW 109P), an earstwhile City VRT/SL3/501 with dual-door bodywork, which is working the trunk route from Bristol. It was one of several transferred to Weston during MAP in January 1981, resulting in City buses working as far away as Taunton!

Allan Macfarlane

Plate 278: Passengers in the Bath region witnessed the resurrection of the Bath fleet-name after over fours years' absence. From its introduction in 1973, until its extinction in 1979 *(see Plates 203 and 227)*, it had only been carried by single deckers and even then, the proportion dimished gradually. From November 1983, however, it was applied to that depot's entire allocation. It is displayed here by No. 8608 (UFX 860S), one of the ex-Southern Vectis convertible VRs that were shortly to lose this half-green, half-white livery. *(See also Plate 270).*

Allan Macfarlane

Plate 279: The new identity chosen for Bristol City vehicles was Citybus, in standard NBC lettering, which many thought to be lacking in inspiration. The eighteen remaining FLFs gained this name in November, but from the end of December their ranks were reduced further by the arrival of new Olympians for the 77/78 service *(see Plate 241)*. Seen here at Henbury, with its new names, and only ten days to live, is 1967 FLF6G, No. 7299 (JHW 67E). After the route's conversion to one-man-operation, in January 1984, route 88 became the last passenger service with a major operator in the entire country to have an FLF allocation.

Allan Macfarlane